· THE ·

SANTA FE

SCHOOL *of* COOKING

··· COOKBOOK ···

· THE ·
...SANTA FE...
SCHOOL *of* COOKING
COOKBOOK

SPIRITED SOUTHWESTERN RECIPES

··· *Susan Curtis* ···

with coauthors Janet Mitchell and Kathi Long
Photographs by Valerie Santagto

GIBBS·SMITH
P
PUBLISHER

SALT LAKE CITY

Dedicated to the memory of M. E. Toliver, my

father, who made all of my dreams possibilities.

First edition
98 97 96 95 5 4 3 2 1

Text copyright © 1995 by Susan D. Curtis and the Santa Fe School of Cooking, Inc.

This is a Peregrine Smith Book, published by
Gibbs Smith, Publisher
P.O. Box 667
Layton, Utah 84041

Design by Traci O'Very Covey, Salt Lake City
Mary Kelly, Editor
Photographs by Valerie Santagto, © 1995 by Valerie Santagto
Cover illustration by Diana Bryer, © 1995 by Diana Bryer

Printed and bound in Korea

Library of Congress Cataloging-in-Publication Data
Curtis, Susan, 1946-
Santa Fe School of Cooking cookbook / Susan Curtis.
    p.   cm.
Includes index.
ISBN 0-87905-619-3 (H : acid-free)
1. Cookery, American—Southwestern style. 2. Cookery—New
Mexico—Santa Fe. 3. Santa Fe (N.M.)—Social life and customs. I.
Santa Fe School of Cooking. II. Title.
TX715.2.S69C88   1995
641.5979—dc20   95-11519

CIP

Contents

Foreword

Santa Fe is indeed a unique ragout of Spanish, Mexican, Native American, and Anglo cultures, piquantly seasoned with sweet and fiery chiles and simmered together for over 400 years. The result is a city with a look, a smell, an attitude, and, above all, a cuisine unlike any other.

As American food becomes ever more homogenized, each outpost battling to preserve genuine local flavor and color becomes increasingly important. Nowhere in the country is that struggle more essential than here in the Southwest.

For 7 years Susan Curtis' Santa Fe School of Cooking has functioned as the major force for educating visiting and resident cooks alike on the richly vibrant cuisine of the Southwest. Susan's determination to operate a professional, authentically regional school means that the book you are holding is the best possible source of ingredient information, recipes, traditional as well as modern cooking methods, and general perspective on this most fascinating of places and its equally fascinating food. From local farmers to internationally acclaimed food writers and restaurant chefs, the voices raised at the school and on these pages are enthusiastically ready to share with you the excitement of Southwest cuisine. Welcome!

Michael McLaughlin, co-author of
The Silver Palate Cookbook

Acknowledgements

First and foremost, this book and all of my endeavors could not be possible without the incredible support of David, Nicole, and Kristen Curtis. Phyllis Toliver, my mother, taught me the meaning of good food and the skill to entertain. For being great sounding boards and full of support, I would like to thank my sister, Lynda Raddon, and my brother, Bud Toliver.

This book is a collaboration of many talented people. Both past and present chefs at the Santa Fe School of Cooking and in particular, Cheryl Alters Jamison, Kathi Long, Janet Mitchell, Jeff Pufal, Todd Sanson, and Bill Weiland. Over the years, all have been instrumental in developing and interpreting recipes and relating cooking techniques to the public. It is not easy to carry on rapport with the class and prepare a meal at the same time. The chefs at the School do an incredibly difficult task with finesse. A special thanks to Kathi Long and Janet Mitchell, contributing authors of this cookbook, and to the staff at the Santa Fe School of Cooking, who have done such a fine job of making guests feel welcome.

Valerie Santagto, photographer and self-declared night person, spent several days rising before the crack of dawn and driving to the farms in northern New Mexico or to Santa Fe Farmer's Market to capture the perfect lighting.

Thanks to the growers and producers of the food being produced in this area. Orlando Casados and his sister Deloris have shared old traditional recipes and food-processing techniques. Thanks to Sylvia Vergara, Patrice Harrison-Inglis, and David Rigsby for taking time out of their busy schedules to share recipes and views on farming as a way of life.

I would like to thank Gibbs Smith for wandering into the School and suggesting we publish a Santa Fe School of Cooking cookbook.

And last, but certainly not least, I would like to thank the wonderful guests of the Santa Fe School of Cooking and Market. Thanks for the years of patronage. So many of you have become good friends and I look forward to meeting more of you.

The Santa Fe Cooking School Staff

INTRODUCTION

The Santa Fe School of Cooking, opened in 1989, blends the traditions, lore, and flavors of the Southwest to offer guests a relaxed approach to learning about northern New Mexico's unique regional cuisine.

Santa Fe School of Cooking instructors, from left to right: **Kathi Long,** author of *Mexican Light* and collaborator on the *Cuisines of Mexico;* **Bill Weiland,** director of the Culinary Arts Program at Santa Fe Community College; **Todd Sanson,** chef, caterer, and owner of Santa Fe Exotix, a gourmet Southwestern food company; **Cheryl Alters Jamison,** coauthor of *Rancho De Chimayo Cookbook, Texas Home Cooking, Smoke and Spice,* and *The Border Cookbook;* **Janet Mitchell,** a lifelong Southwest resident, home economics and cooking instructor, and caterer; **Jeff Pufal,** executive chef at Camelot, Decathlon Club, and Pecos River Learning Center; and **Susan Curtis.**

The Origins of Santa Fe Cuisine

The Native Americans of northern New Mexico were people with a strong sense of community and a highly refined ability to live in harmony with their surroundings. They grew crops using canals and ditches to take advantage of the perennial rivers and undependable precipitation. In concert with the seasonal rhythms, they grew, harvested, and stored corn, beans, pumpkins, and gourds. Wild harvests were part of the native diet, including the roots of wild onions, milkweed and seed pods, and nuts from oaks and piñons. Meat from mountain sheep, deer, squirrel, prairie dog, mountain lion, badger, fox, and field mouse was eaten on special occasions. The pueblos never domesticated animals for food.

The first Spanish explorers arrived in the summer of 1540, led by General don Francisco Vasquez de Coronado. The town of Santa Fe is believed to have been established as early as 1607. It became the seat for Spanish colonial government and remained the seat of government for over two hundred years. During this time, the Spanish colonists dispersed into the countryside, and traditions from Spain and Mexico were blended with those of the native population to define a new regional culture and cuisine. Fields of wheat, oats, barley, chile, onions, peas, and new varieties of beans redefined the landscape of the region. Orchards of peaches, apricots, and apples extended the peripheries of the towns and ranches. Cattle and sheep grazed in the hills surrounding the city.

In the late twentieth century, "the city different" has come to represent a unique convergence of ancient traditions, diverse cultures, commerce, and the arts. This diversity and the blend of old and new is nowhere more evident than in the cuisine. Santa Fe offers a magical mix of traditional New Mexican food and contemporary Southwestern cuisine. The Santa Fe School of Cooking reflects this diversity of New Mexican culture and its food, past and present.

What the School is All About

The heart and soul of the School is the agriculture upon which the food is based. Many of the traditional methods of growing and processing regional foods—posole, atole, chicos—are almost lost arts. The Cooking School serves as a vehicle to expose and sustain traditional lifestyles. It introduces the unique cuisine of this region to cooks from around the country, and even from around the world. Beginners, accomplished home cooks, and professional chefs all come to the School to learn the basics of Santa Fe cuisine, to improve their skills, or to find new inspiration. The School offers classes for cooks at every level and gives everyone who attends a chance to connect with the Santa Fe food community.

And that community is very much a part of the Cooking School experience. Classes are by no means confined to the classroom; instead the School offers an in-depth look at the food and the people of the Southwest. One class travels to the Santa Fe Farmer's Market. Our culinary tours include visits to small farms, tortilla and tamale factories, local breweries, and to El Rancho de los Golondrinas, a living Spanish Colonial museum, where participants watch bread being baked in traditional horno (adobe beehive) ovens. Guests are encouraged to experience the complete chain of regional cuisine from the seed, to observing the harvesting and processing of the unique agricultural products and utilizing the fresh or dried forms in Southwestern recipes.

The Santa Fe School of Cooking offers a wide range of classes, from the authentic, traditional cuisine to the contemporary to the health-conscious, all in a relaxed, casual atmosphere. Class offerings at the School include traditional New Mexican favorites such as tortillas, chile sauces, and enchiladas. These classes focus on recipes and techniques for processing agricultural products which are essentially unchanged from techniques used years ago. Other classes, such as Mexican Light Cooking (our fastest-growing class) and the Southwest Vegetarian class, reflect more modern interests. Several contemporary menus combine techniques and foods from other parts of the world with products indigenous to this area. Classes in Mexican Cuisine (distinctively different from New Mexican), Tapas, and Southwestern Breakfast are also offered. New classes are continually being added. Our chefs provide culinary tips and techniques, unlock mysteries surrounding New Mexico's renowned red and green chiles, and offer up a liberal dose of area culture and history, as well as recommendations on where to eat and shop. In addition to our talented resident chefs, special classes feature cookbook authors including Deborah Madison and Jacqueline Higuera McMahan or restaurant chefs like Mark Miller.

The Cooking School Market

Like the Cooking School, the Santa Fe School of Cooking Market promotes regional agriculture and food products. Many of the items used in the cooking classes such as chicos, posole, atole (blue corn meal), and chiles are difficult to find, so we offer them here at the School. Products raised and/or produced by what I consider to be the best local farmers are packaged under the Santa Fe School of Cooking label. A visit to the Market is a sensual delight in the tastes, sights, and smells of these products. Samples of numerous foods produced in New Mexico are always available. Like the city itself, the people who grow and process the foods from around New Mexico are diverse and interesting. Visitors to the Market are able to meet these suppliers on Vendors' Days, when we offer free cooking demonstrations and suppliers instruct guests on how to use their products.

Bring the Santa Fe School of Cooking Into Your Home

Now with this book, you can bring the Santa Fe School of Cooking experience right into your own home. I've included recipes from every class, so you get the full range of the School's offerings. I've included tips, techniques, and ingredient information that guests at the school receive. And I've introduced many of the people of the Santa Fe food community—the farmers, the processors, and the guest chefs—so that, when you come to the Santa Fe School of Cooking, you'll already be old friends.

You Can Use These Recipes Every Day

I've included special-occasion recipes here: Roast Turkey with Mole Poblano, and that traditional Christmas favorite, Tamales. But here also are recipes for every day of the year. Serve Green Chile Stew or Red Chile Mashed Potatoes for family suppers. Entertain Santa Fe style, with Chile-Marinated Pork Tenderloin with Roasted Pineapple Salsa. Take Birria and Biscochitos (the state cookie of New Mexico) on a picnic or outing. Looking for something light? Fiesta Cole Slaw contains no oil at all, and Fresh Fruit with Tequila Lime Sauce makes a luscious, low-fat dessert. Prefer vegetarian? Try Stuffed Poblano Chile with Red Chile Sauce, a sophisticated blend of goat cheese, pine nuts, and raisins in a chile chocolate sauce. This eclectic collection of Southwestern recipes is so versatile, it lets you serve the full range of Santa Fe cuisine on occasions of every sort. Whether you are a professional chef or a novice cook, you'll find in The *Santa Fe School of Cooking Cookbook* all the recipes, and all the expertise, that make the school so popular.

Buen Provecho,
Susan Curtis

Chiles

All ABOUT CHILES

The importance of chiles in the culture and cuisine of Santa Fe and the Southwest is such that it is often said we have only two seasons—red and green. Chiles have been cultivated and used for at least 1,000 years by the Southwest Pueblo Indians and their ancestors, contributing flavor and piquancy to the cuisines of many civilizations. The popularity of chile and cuisines using chile as an ingredient continues to rise. The largest producer of chiles in the United States is New Mexico, where the greatest consumption of chiles also occurs.

The large majority of the chiles are grown in the southern part of the state where there is a long, warm growing season. The northern part of the state, in the Chimayo and Dixon valleys, has historically been known for its particularly flavorful red chiles.

Types of Chiles

Confusion sometimes reigns over the use and categorization of chiles. Over two hundred varieties of chiles have been positively identified, and many of these same chiles are known by different names in different localities. To help you sort it out, types of chiles—fresh, dried, and powdered—frequently called for in these recipes are listed and described here.

ANCHO: The ancho chile is highly esteemed in Mexico where it is probably the most commonly used dried pepper. Ancho, the dried form of the green poblano, means "wide" and is a reddish-brown, flat, heart-shaped chile. Anchos vary in pungency from almost mild to medium, with smoky flavors reminiscent of coffee, prunes, and tobacco. For the "chile novice," this chile is a good one with which to begin chile exploration.

ANCHO POWDER: Ground form of the ancho pod.

CASCABEL CHILE: A dried, dark reddish brown chile with smooth, tough skin and a round shape about 1 1/2 inches in diameter. In Spanish, cascabel means "rattle," and the chile is so named because of the sound the seeds make inside the dried pepper. Medium hot with a slightly acidic quality, this chile is often used in uncooked table salsas.

CHILE CARIBE: Crushed form of New Mexican dried red chile pods along with the seeds.

CHIPOTLES: Dried and smoked form of a fresh jalapeño chile which is dusty brown in color. It is ridged, with wrinkly skin measuring about 2 to 2 1/2 inches long and about 3/4 to 1 inch wide. The chipotle has a rich, smoky, tobaccolike flavor with a very pronounced heat.

CHIPOTLES IN ADOBO: Canned chipotle chiles in a sauce of tomatoes, vinegar, garlic, onion, and spices. Until recently, chipotles in adobo were imported from Mexico, but they have begun to be processed within the United States.

DE ARBOL: A dried, bright red chile measuring 2 to 3 inches long and related to the cayenne chile. It is very hot with intense flavor.

GUAJILLO: Dried red chile pod similar in look to a dried New Mexican pod but smaller and smoother in texture. It has an earthy flavor.

JALAPEÑO: Fresh, small, thick-fleshed green chile approximately 2 inches long and 1 inch wide. It is the most popular hot green chile.

MORITAS: Another type of dried, smoked jalapeño chile which is deep red to red-brown in color. It measures 1 to 2 inches long and about 3/8 inches wide.

NEW MEXICO GREEN CHILE: Fresh New Mexican variety of chile in its green form, measuring about 4 to 6 inches long. There are a variety of types of New Mexican chiles distinguished by heat level from the mild (New Mexico 6-4) to hot (Barker). When New Mexican green chile is called for, it is assumed the chile has been roasted and peeled.

NEW MEXICO RED PODS: The form of the green chile that has ripened to its red state and dried. The traditional method for storing these chiles is to tie them in a long bunch called a ristra.

NEW MEXICO OR CHIMAYO CHILE POWDER: Dried version of the New Mexican Green chile which has been ripened (turned red) and ground into powder without additional ingredients.

MULATO: A type of poblano chile, dried, browner in color than the ancho chile and slightly smokier, but without the depth. It is one of the three chiles (ancho, mulato, pasilla) used in traditional Mole Poblano.

PASILLA: Also call Chile Negro. Pasilla, a dried chile, translates as "little raisin." It is brownish-black in color, wrinkled, long, and tapered. It is one of the chiles used in a Mole Poblano.

POBLANO: Fresh form of the ancho chile measuring 3 to 4 inches. This is a good chile for chiles rellenos due to its size and the thickness of its flesh. A dark green color, the poblano is usually charred and peeled to enhance its full flavor.

SERRANO: Fresh, small green chile, cylindrical in shape and measuring approximately 1 to 2 inches long and 1/2 to 3/4 inch in width. It is a crisp, hot chile used extensively in salsas.

Availability of Chiles

GROWING CHILES

The perennial chile plants are relatively easy to grow and produce amazing numbers of pods on just a few plants in a very small garden area. They will grow almost anywhere in the United States but are the most productive in areas that are warm, with a long growing season. If you want to have fresh chiles all year long, chiles can also be grown indoors in pots in warm and sunny spots. Seedlings can be purchased at nurseries in the spring, or seeds can be ordered from the sources listed on page 173.

Fresh chiles such as jalapeño, serrano, and Anaheim (similar, but not as hot nor flavorful as the New Mexican variety) are available today in many supermarkets that offer a large variety of fresh produce. Fresh New Mexican green chiles can be ordered during harvest time (approximately August to September) through the Cooking School with direct shipment from the farm. If fresh chiles, our number one preference at the cooking school, are unavailable, frozen or canned chiles can be substituted in certain recipes. However, we do not heartily recommend canned chiles as their taste and texture is quite different from that of fresh chiles. When selecting fresh green chiles, choose pods that are firm to the touch and heavy for the size, with smooth, shiny skins. Chile powder, composed of one hundred percent dried ground chiles, should posses a deep, rich color and a strong and earthy aroma. The freshest chile powders will be slightly lumpy in consistency, an indication that the natural oils have not evaporated. When purchasing a chile ristra for cooking purposes, rather than for a decorative use, make certain that it has not been varnished, and that the pods are pest and mold free.

Health Aspects

Medical research is beginning to support some of the claims of numerous folk remedies for the efficacy of chile peppers in treating a wide variety of health conditions. Studies are underway to explore chiles' facility to reduce the risk of heart attack, prevent cancer, aid in digestion, and reduce obesity. Researchers have already developed a medicine containing the capsaicin from chiles which is the only effective treatment for the pain associated with the nerve disorder shingles. In 1828, Albert Szent-Gyorgyi, a professor at the University of Szeged in Hungary, began the first work with vitamin C by studying paprika, a chile pepper. Today we know that chile peppers are excellent sources of both vitamins A and C. The fresh green pods contain twice the amount of vitamin C as citrus, retaining a high percentage even when canned or frozen. However, the vitamin C content is lessened by about half in the dried red pods and powder. The vitamin A content increases one hundred times as the pods turn from green to red. Vitamin A is extremely stable and is unaffected by cooking, freezing, or time. Chiles are cholesterol-free, low in calories and sodium, and are good sources of folic acid, potassium, and vitamin E, making them good for you as well as good to eat. Claims of people being "chile addicts" and needing their daily chile fixes do have some scientific basis. Upon ingesting chiles, the brain is stimulated to release endorphins, which are morphinelike natural painkillers that produce a sense of well-being.

HEAT AND HANDLING

The best known quality of chiles is their heat, which is created by the capsaicin, a potent, odorless, and tasteless alkaloid that remains unaffected by the cooking and freezing processes. No matter how enjoyable this fiery sensation is for the taste buds, it can pose a problem to your skin and eyes. When handling chile pods, never touch your eyes or contact lenses. Wearing rubber gloves to process or chop chiles is recommended, especially for people who have sensitive skin. Because capsaicin is oil soluble but not miscible in water, washing your hands in water does little to ease the burning sensation. To relieve a burning sensation, "wash" your hands in vegetable oil or in a solution of 5 parts water and 1 part chlorine bleach.

Roasting and Peeling the Fresh Pods

Fresh green New Mexican chiles require blistering or roasting to separate the tough transparent skin from the flesh of the chile so that the skin can be removed. This process also imparts a smoky aroma and flavor to the chiles. There are several methods that you can use. Our favorite variation is to roast them over the gas flame of a stove on the El Asador (page 118) or on a charcoal grill over a hot fire. The chiles can also be placed in a single layer on a baking sheet and blackened under the broiler. Turn the chiles as they blister and darken so that the skins are evenly charred. Remove chiles from the broiler and immediately place the roasted chiles in a paper or plastic bag to steam for ten minutes, or until cool enough to handle. To peel, hold the chile by the stem and gently peel the charred skin from the flesh. If stubborn particles of blackened skin cling to the chile, hold the chile under cold, running water as you peel. If the chile is to be used whole, as in chiles rellenos, leave the stem end intact, slit the chile lengthwise, and with your fingers carefully pull out the seeds. Store the chiles in the refrigerator if you are not using them immediately. If you want to freeze the chiles, there is no need to peel first as they will peel quite easily after being frozen. Whatever form of chiles (whole, strips, or chopped) you choose to freeze, consider packaging some of them in smaller quantities rather than having to chop apart a large frozen block when only a small amount is needed. Frozen chiles keep well for at least a year.

Jams & vinegars made by Sylvia Vergara of La Carreta

APPETIZERS:

Fiesta Fare

The Santa Fe life style is casual and relaxed, and both dining and entertaining often revolve around small snacks or appetizers. At some of Santa Fe's most popular restaurants, people often eat at the bar rather than in the dining room, making a meal of appetizers. At the School, we offer a Tapas class. Tapas originated in Spain, but our class focuses on appetizers utilizing ingredients indigenous to northern New Mexico. The spirit of the food is the same and the recipes provide an

informal approach to entertaining. At the welcome receptions for our culinary tours, we serve a meal of hearty appetizers while Rubin Romero, a well-known local guitarist, performs. This combination of fiesta foods, celebration beverages, and lively music introduces guests to the ambiance of Santa Fe. And it seems to bring people together much more quickly than a formal sit-down dinner ever could.

Blue Corn Pancakes

**YIELD: 26 TO 28
2-INCH PANCAKES**

4 large eggs

2 cups buttermilk

1 1/2 cups blue cornmeal (See Blue Corn)

1 cup all-purpose flour

1 tablespoon baking powder

1 tablespoon sugar

1 cup fresh corn kernels, or frozen, thawed

1/2 cup diced red bell pepper

2 green onions, thinly sliced

1 teaspoon minced garlic

3 tablespoons coarsely chopped fresh cilantro

1/2 teaspoon salt

2 tablespoons melted butter

This is a recipe from our Tapas class. It has been used a number of times as an appetizer for the cocktail parties. It is a unique and wonderful start for a dinner, too. The pancakes can be served with a variety of sauces. However, at the school, we usually serve it with Green Chile Chutney. (See page 109 for recipe)

1. In a large bowl, combine the eggs and buttermilk and whisk thoroughly. Slowly stir in the dry ingredients and whisk until no lumps appear. Add the remaining ingredients, stirring to distribute evenly.
2. Preheat a cast iron griddle or a non-stick frying pan over medium-high heat and wipe the griddle with vegetable oil or spray with vegetable cooking spray. Using a 1-ounce ladle, pour ladles-full of the batter onto the cooking surface and cook about 1 1/2 minutes on each side or until lightly browned.
3. Place cooked pancakes on a baking sheet and keep warm until ready to serve.

BLUE CORN

The ground meal made from blue corn is nuttier in flavor, higher in protein, and lower in starch than the meal made from either white or yellow corn, and it produces a more fragile tortilla. The color of the kernel and the meal is gray-blue. If the kernel is popped, the popped corn is white. The Native Americans cultivated blue corn thousands of years ago for use in their ceremonies honoring the regeneration of Mother Earth. Today, blue corn has become quite popular and is considered a novelty in most parts of the world.

Beef Salpicon

SERVES 12 TO 14

SALPICON DRESSING:

1 7-ounce can chipotle chiles in adobo sauce

1 cup extra-virgin olive oil

2/3 cup fresh lime juice

1/4 cup cider vinegar

2 garlic cloves, minced

Salt and coarse-ground black pepper to taste

SALPICON SALAD:

3 1/2 pounds shredded smoked beef brisket (See Smoking Beef Brisket)

4 small red-ripe tomatoes, preferably Romas or Italian plum, diced

2 ripe avocados, preferably Haas, diced

1 large red bell pepper, diced

1 medium red onion, diced

6 ounces Monterey Jack cheese, grated

2/3 cup chopped fresh cilantro

6 medium radishes, grated

1 head romaine, shredded

Once or twice during the year, we have a four- or five-day culinary tour during which we visit local farms, wineries, breweries, and restaurants in addition to having many cooking classes. Cheryl Alters Jamison developed this recipe for our welcome reception. This wonderful dish can be served with tortillas chips for an appetizer, or as a main dish.*

1. Combine all the dressing ingredients in a blender or food processor and process until well combined.
2. In a large bowl, combine the brisket with half to three-quarters of the salad dressing. Refrigerate for at least 2 hours, or up to overnight.
3. Remove the meat from the refrigerator and let it sit at room temperature for about 30 minutes. Add the remaining ingredients to the brisket and toss well. Drizzle on more dressing as you wish, keeping in mind it will increase the salad's heat level. Serve immediately.

* This recipe appears in *Smoke & Spice*
(Harvard Common Press, 1994) by Cheryl and Bill Jamison.

SMOKING BEEF BRISKET

"The key to real barbecue is long, slow smoking over a wood fire. You need sufficient heat to cook the food, the main difference from smoke curing, but much lower temperatures than with conventional high-heat grilling. The food should never actually come in contact with burning wood, but rather be cooked and flavored by the fire's cloud of smoke. As we explain in detail in *Smoke & Spice*, the right equipment is essential but a lot of ways will work. Home smoking options include water smokers, stove-top smokers, wood-fired pits, and kettle grills. The rapid development of new equipment, a virtual revolution of recent years, allows anyone to get the smoky resonance long associated with real, old-fashioned 'Bar-B-Q.' The technique can be applied to traditional meats like beef brisket and pork ribs, and to seafood, poultry, and even vegetables, as well." —*Cheryl Alters Jamison and Bill Jamison*

Chama River
Salmon Tamale

SERVES 6

1 1/2 pounds fresh salmon, trimmed of all ligaments, membrane, and fat and cut into chunks

2 cups heavy cream

1 teaspoon salt

1 teaspoon white pepper

1 egg

1 cup corn masa for tamales (See p. 100)

12 dried corn husks

John Rivera Sedlar, of Abiquiu Restaurant located in Los Angeles and San Francisco, contributed this recipe. He grew up in Abiquiu and Santa Fe but presently lives on the West Coast. John prepared this dish when he was a guest chef at the Cooking School during the 1994 Wine & Chile Fiesta, which is an annual city-wide event the last weekend of September. Fifty local restaurants join forces with fifty national and international wineries to establish that wine does indeed go with Southwestern food and to celebrate Santa Fe's cuisine. There are a number of activities ranging from wine dinners, big bottle auctions, and food tastings to wine seminars and cooking classes.

1. Put the salmon, cream, salt, and pepper in a processor and process for 1 minute, stopping a few times to scrape the bowl. Add the egg and process 1 minute more, to make a firm, dense mousse mixture. It should be free of any ligaments. If there are any visible, press the mixture with a rubber spatula through a fine sieve.
2. For each tamale, place a 4 x 5-inch sheet of plastic wrap on the work surface. Spread a 1/4-inch thick layer of fresh masa in a 1 1/2 x 3-inch rectangle in the center of the sheet. On top of the fresh masa, spread a 1/2-inch thick layer of the mousse mixture. Cut a 1 1/2 x 3-inch rectangle from each of 6 corn husks and place it on top. Bring the plastic wrap up and around the husk to seal the tamale in a neat package. Set the tamales aside.

XEREZ VINEGAR SAUCE:

1/2 cup Xerez vinegar

1 cup dry white wine

1 teaspoon salt

1/2 teaspoon white pepper

2 shallots, peeled and left whole

1/4 cup heavy cream

12 tablespoons unsalted butter, softened

1 cup peeled, seeded and diced tomatoes, for garnish

1. Put the vinegar, wine, salt, pepper, and shallots in a medium saucepan and bring them to a boil over medium-high heat. Cook at a low, rolling boil until the liquid has been reduced to 1/4 cup, about 15 minutes.

2. Add the cream and boil until the liquid is reduced to 1/4 cup, about 5 minutes more. With a wire whisk, briskly whisk in the butter in small pieces until it is fully incorporated. Sieve the sauce, cover it, and keep it warm.

ASSEMBLY:

Cook the tamales in a steamer for about 9 minutes, or until firm. Take them from the steamer and remove plastic wrap. Place some of the sauce on each of 6 plates. Place 2 corn husks on the sauce and place a tamale in each of the corn husks. Sprinkle with the diced tomato for garnish.

THE KOKANEE SALMON

This landlocked form of the sockeye salmon is the only salmon species found in all of New Mexico. It was introduced to the Chama River back in the 1960s and has been a favorite catch of local fishermen since that time. The flesh of this fresh water fish is milder in flavor and somewhat lighter in color than the seafaring salmon.

Guacamole

YIELD: ABOUT 3 CUPS

3 ripe avocados, about 6 ounces each (See Ripening Avocados)

3/4 cup finely diced white onion

3/4 cup diced ripe plum tomatoes

2 to 3 tablespoons finely chopped serrano chiles, to taste (jalapeño or roasted and peeled New Mexican chiles may be substituted)

1/2 cup coarsely chopped fresh cilantro

2 tablespoons freshly squeezed lime juice

2 teaspoons coarse salt, to taste

As many times as guacamole is served in Santa Fe, one would think avocados were indigenous to New Mexico. They are not, but guacamole has become a staple as an appetizer and garnish to New Mexican and Southwestern dishes. The quality of guacamole is dependent upon the quality and ripeness of the avocados. When available, I prefer Haas avocados, which are a black, rough-skinned avocado.

1. Cut each avocado in half and remove the pit. Cut the halves in half and carefully peel off the black skin.
2. Cut the quarters into chunks and place in a medium bowl. Mash the avocado with a fork and stir in the onion, tomatoes, chiles, and cilantro. Season the mixture with lime juice and salt. Keep covered with plastic wrap pressed against the surface of the guacamole until ready to serve.

RIPENING AVOCADOS

It is often difficult to find an avocado at the market possessing just the right degree of ripeness for your intended use. To hasten ripening, remove the stem end from the avocado and bury the avocado in a canister of flour for a day or two. Unless your avocado was rock-hard to begin with, you will have a usable avocado.

Chicken & Jalapeño Quesadillas

SERVES 8

16 8-inch flour tortillas

1 pound Monterey Jack cheese, grated

6 to 8 fresh jalapeño chiles, seeded and thinly sliced

1 pound cooked chicken, shredded

3 cups shredded red cabbage

2 cups sour cream

2 cups Salsa Fresca (page 119)

There are many versions of quesadillas with different fillings and a variety of cooking methods. Try experimenting with corn tortillas instead of flour. If you are not concerned with calories and fat, frying quesadillas in oil is a delicious variation. Fillings range from breakfast ingredients (eggs, potatoes, etc.) to vegetables or smoked meats. Experiment to find the type of quesadilla you most enjoy. The following quesadillas recipe is one which we have used for our Traditional New Mexican III class.

1. Preheat the oven to 350 degrees.
2. Place one tortilla on a flat surface and cover it with cheese. Sprinkle jalapeños and chicken over the cheese and cover with more cheese. Place another tortilla over the cheese and put the finished product on a baking sheet. Repeat with remaining tortillas.
3. Bake the quesadillas in the oven for 10 to 12 minutes, or until the cheese melts. Remove from the oven and cut each quesadilla into 4 pieces. Transfer the pieces to serving plates and garnish with cabbage, sour cream, and Salsa Fresca.

CABBAGE

Cabbage has been used as a green, such as in this quesadilla recipe, by New Mexicans of Spanish and Native American extraction since early times. Availability, and tolerance for long-term, unrefrigerated storage made cabbage a natural greens choice. The early cooks devised many different uses for this hearty vegetable.

Open-faced Quesadillas with Goat Cheese and Roasted Peppers

SERVES 8

8 8-inch flour tortillas

1/2 pound grated Monterey Jack Cheese

1/4 pound crumbled goat cheese

3 tablespoons olive oil

1 medium onion, thinly sliced

2 medium garlic cloves, peeled and thinly sliced

1 red bell pepper, roasted, peeled, seeded, and cut into thin strips

1 to 2 fresh poblano or New Mexico green chiles, roasted, peeled, seeded, and cut into thin strips

Salt and freshly ground black pepper to taste

Fresh herbs (optional)

1. Preheat the oven to 350 degrees.
2. Place the tortillas on a flat surface and sprinkle them with 1/4 cup of Jack cheese. Sprinkle 1 tablespoon of goat cheese over the Jack cheese.
3. Heat the olive oil in a large skillet over medium-high heat. Add the onion and sauté until it is translucent. Add the garlic and continue to cook until the garlic is lightly golden.
4. Add the red and yellow bell pepper strips and the chile strips and combine thoroughly. Season to taste.
5. Divide the sautéed ingredients among the tortillas and top with more of the cheese.
6. Bake the quesadillas in the oven for 10 to 12 minutes, or until the cheese melts. Remove from the oven and cut each quesadilla into 4 pieces. Serve warm.

Chipotle Shrimp with Corn Cakes and Pico de Gallo Salsa

CHIPOTLE SHRIMP:

YIELD: 6 SERVINGS

1 1/2 pounds medium shrimp

3 tablespoons butter

1 cup softened butter

4 1/2 tablespoons canned chipotle chiles, puréed

1 1/2 dozen Corn Cakes

2 green onions, chopped

1 cup Pico de Gallo Salsa

Mark Miller opened the Coyote Cafe in Santa Fe in 1987, an event which immediately focused national and international attention on the cuisine of the "city different." Because of the attention that Coyote Cafe received, Santa Fe moved to the forefront of contemporary Southwest cuisine. Over the years, Mark has taught several times at the Santa Fe School of Cooking. His background in anthropology and skill in cooking make his classes extremely informative and interesting.*

1. Peel the shrimp. On a griddle or in a frying pan, cook the shrimp in 3 tablespoons butter over low heat for about 5 minutes, turning them once.
2. To prepare chipotle butter, roughly purée together the softened butter and 1 1/2 tablespoons chipotle purée and set aside at room temperature.
3. Place 3 corn cakes on each plate. Place shrimp on top of the cakes and spread the chipotle butter liberally over the shrimp. Sprinkle the chopped green onions over the shrimp. Serve the Pico de Gallo Salsa at the side of the corn cakes.

*These three recipes for a classic appetizer at Coyote Cafe are from the *Coyote Cafe* cookbook (Ten Speed Press, 1989).

CORN CAKES:

YIELD: 18 TO 20 CORN CAKES

3/4 cup all-purpose flour

1/2 cup coarse cornmeal (polenta)

1/2 teaspoon baking powder

1/2 teaspoon baking soda

1 teaspoon salt

1 teaspoon sugar

1 1/4 cups buttermilk

2 tablespoons melted butter

1 egg, beaten

1 cup fresh corn kernels

2 green onions, chopped

1. Place the dry ingredients in a bowl and mix together. In a large bowl, whisk the buttermilk and butter together and then whisk in the egg. Gradually add the dry ingredients to the liquid and whisk until thoroughly incorporated.

2. Purée 1/2 cup of the corn, and fold it into the batter along with the whole kernels and green onions. Add a little buttermilk if necessary to thin the mixture.

3. Using a nonstick pan over medium heat, ladle corn cake batter and form 3-inch cakes. Cook until golden brown (about 2 1/2 minutes on each side).

PICO DE GALLO SALSA:

YIELD: ABOUT 2 CUPS

2 tablespoons diced onion

2 cups tomatoes chopped into 1/4 inch cubes

2 serrano chiles, finely chopped

2 tablespoons finely chopped cilantro

2 teaspoons sugar

1/4 cup Mexican beer

2 teaspoons salt

juice of 1 lime

1. Put onion in a strainer, rinse with hot water, and drain.

2. Combine all ingredients and mix well. Let sit in the refrigerator for at least 30 minutes before serving.

Salted Pecans with Red Chile

2 cups whole pecans

1 teaspoon olive oil

1 teaspoon kosher salt

Ground red New Mexico chile, to taste

Deborah Madison is a guest chef at the Cooking School and author of *The Greens Cookbook* (Bantam 1987) and *The Savory Way* (Bantam 1990). She recommends serving the nuts with sherry, olives, and a simple crudite. Keep a bagful on hand in the freezer for unexpected guests.

1. Preheat the oven to 300 degrees.
2. Toss the nuts with the oil and roast until fragrant, about 25 minutes. Stir a few times so that they toast evenly.
3. When done, add salt and chile and swish nuts around. Taste and add more salt or chile, if desired.

PECANS IN NEW MEXICO

Native pecan trees are reported to have saved the lives of starving, sixteenth-century Spanish explorers with Cabeza De Vaca. Today, New Mexico has approximately 25,000 acres of pecan trees, mostly in the fertile Mesilla Valley in the southern part of the state. This region produces excellent pecans and makes New Mexico the third largest producer of pecans in the United States.

Sautéed Shrimp with Orange-Chipotle Honey Mustard Sauce

SERVES 6

2 to 3 tablespoons vegetable oil

2 pounds (32 to 36) shrimp, peeled and deveined

1 1/2 cups Orange Chipotle Honey-Mustard Sauce

Chef Bill Weiland developed this recipe for our Tapas class. Shrimp seem to be everyone's favorite and this dish is very popular. The smoky citrus flavor of the sauce is a delicious compliment to the sautéed shrimp.

1. Heat the oil in a large, heavy skillet over medium-high heat. Add one quarter of the shrimp and sauté until just cooked through, about 2 to 3 minutes. Continue with the next quarter, and so on, until all the shrimp have been cooked.

2. Place the cooked shrimp in a large bowl and pour the sauce over them. Toss to combine well and serve the shrimp warm.

ORANGE CHIPOTLE HONEY-MUSTARD SAUCE:

YIELD: 1 1/2 CUPS

1 6-ounce can frozen orange juice concentrate, thawed

2 to 3 tablespoons chipotle chiles and juice from a 7-ounce can of Chipotle Chiles in Adobo Sauce

2 tablespoons honey

2 tablespoons Dijon mustard

1 teaspoon minced garlic

1/3 cup coarsely chopped fresh cilantro, packed

2 tablespoons fresh lime juice

1/2 teaspoon salt or to taste

2 to 3 tablespoons vegetable oil

1. Place all ingredients in a blender and purée until smooth.

Smoked Jalapeño Shrimp

SERVES 4

MARINADE:

1/3 cup pickled
jalapeño slices

1/2 cup juice from
pickled jalapeños

Juice of 2 limes

4 tablespoons corn oil,
preferably unrefined

2 tablespoons minced
cilantro

4 green onions, sliced

3 garlic cloves, minced

1 pound large shrimp (24
to 30 shrimp per pound)

1/2 cup unsalted seafood
stock or water

This recipe has proven to be a favorite at our welcome receptions for the culinary tours. It was developed by one of the School's chefs, Cheryl Alters Jamison.*

1. In a food processor or blender, purée the marinade ingredients.
2. Peel the shrimp, leaving the tails on. Clean and, if you like, devein them. Place the shrimp in a large, nonreactive pan or bowl.
3. One hour before you plan to begin smoking the shrimp, pour the marinade over them.
4. Remove the shrimp from the marinade, and, when the temperature is about 180 degrees F to 200 degrees F, place them in the pit on a small grill rack.
5. Add the stock or water to the remaining marinade, boil, and baste the shrimp at intervals of about 10 minutes. The shrimp should cook in about 30 minutes, but watch them carefully. They are ready when opaque, slightly firm, and light pink on the exterior. Serve them immediately, or wrap them in foil to keep them warm for up to 45 minutes.

*This recipe appears in *Texas Home Cooking* (Harvard Common Press, 1993), written by Cheryl Alters Jamison and Bill Jamison.

Southwestern Gravlax

SERVES 15 TO 20

2 pounds salmon fillet, pin bones removed, skin left on

1/4 cup kosher (coarse) salt

1/4 cup sugar

3 tablespoons ground Chimayo red chile

1 bunch fresh cilantro, washed and thoroughly dried

A traditional Scandinavian dish, gravlax is fresh salmon, cured with salt, sugar, and pepper, layered with fresh dill and weighted for several days, until it is rather translucent with a wonderful salty-sweet, "salmon-y" flavor. It is thinly sliced and served with different types of mustard sauces. Here in this recipe we have adapted the traditional method to use more contemporary ingredients.

1. Cut the salmon in half lengthwise.
2. Combine the salt, sugar, and chile in a small bowl. Rub liberally over the salmon halves.
3. Roughly chop the cilantro and spread it over one of the half fillets. Place one fillet on top of the other and cover with plastic wrap.
4. Place the package in a pan with another pan on top. Place added weight in the top pan so the fillets are pressed together. Refrigerate the salmon for at least 3 days.
5. To serve: Thinly slice salmon for serving on slices of buttered rye bread, chile brioche, or any coarse, peasantlike bread. Garnish with minced white onion, capers, and cilantro sour cream.

Tortilla Roll-ups

SERVES 6 TO 8

11 ounces cream cheese, softened

1 teaspoon grainy Dijon mustard

1 tablespoon ground New Mexico red chile, or 1/4 teaspoon cayenne

1 to 2 pickled jalapeño chiles, plus 1 tablespoon juice from the jar

3 green onions, minced

1/2 cup sliced black olives or stuffed green olives

2 tablespoons chopped jalapeño-pickled carrots

2 tablespoons minced cilantro

6 very fresh 10-inch flour tortillas

2 cups slivered red leaf or other colorful lettuce

1/2 pound paper-thin slices of smoked turkey

This basic recipe is one of Jacquie Higuera McMahan's favorites. However, it changes depending on what is available. Its versatility and simplicity will make this a standard in your household too. Jacquie lives in southern California and has been a guest chef at the Santa Fe School of Cooking. She has authored *California Rancho Cooking, Healthy Fiesta, The Red and Green Chile Cookbook, Salsa, Mexican Breakfast,* and, coming out soon, *The Chipotle Chile Cookbook.* All books are published by the Olive Press.

1. Place the cream cheese in a bowl. Blend in the mustard, ground chile, pickled jalapeños and juice, green onions, olives, pickled carrots, and cilantro. Taste and adjust seasonings.
2. Spread equal amounts of the mixture over each tortilla. Top with a little lettuce and gently press it into the cheese. Arrange 2 or 3 slices of turkey over the lettuce on each tortilla. Tightly roll up the tortillas and wrap each in plastic wrap. Refrigerate 2 to 3 hours.
3. Just before serving, cut each roll into 6 slices.

VARIATIONS:

In place of the lettuce and smoked turkey, try flat-leaf spinach and thin slices of smoked ham or salami. Or try substituting finely diced red onion and roasted red or yellow peppers with shredded fresh basil for the green onions, olives, and cilantro. And, if you want a less spicy result, omit the jalapeño-pickled carrots.

Zucchini and Green Chile Tamales

MAKES ABOUT 24 TAMALES, 4 OUNCES EACH, OR ABOUT 12 MAIN-DISH SERVINGS

Pork tamales are very common in Santa Fe and northern New Mexico, particularly at Christmas. Freshly made tamales are available at almost all grocery stores throughout the year, but making tamales is an activity many families enjoy. Because of the numerous steps involved in making tamales, it is frequently a social event, with friends and family invited to participate. Tamales can be filled with a variety of stuffings such as smoked duck, salmon, a variety of vegetables, and even dessert fillings. After you have the concept of tamale-making down, experiment to find a filling that suits your taste. We have made a variety of tamales at the School. The Zucchini and Green Chile Tamale is consistently a favorite. Leona Tiede of Leona's de Chimaya, a tortilla and tamale factory, developed this recipe and shared her skills with us at the Cooking School when she taught a tamale-making class. She developed a vegetarian tamale after receiving a number of requests from the International Sikh community located near Chimayo where Leona's is located. Visiting Leona'a factory is always a must on our culinary tours. Tamales and tortillas are available by mail. See the Supplier List on page 173.

FILLING:

1 cup roasted, peeled green chiles, preferably New Mexico or Anaheim, fresh or frozen

1/4 cup water

3 pounds zucchini, grated

2 teaspoons minced garlic

Salt to taste

TAMALES:

1 6-ounce package dried corn husks

6 cups masa harina (See p. 100)

1 2/3 cups canola or vegetable oil

5 1/2 cups water, or more as needed

1 tablespoon salt

1. In a small, heavy saucepan, simmer the green chiles and water over very low heat until the chiles have darkened in color and most of the liquid has evaporated. Cool.

2. Pour the green chiles into a large bowl and add the zucchini, garlic, and salt and mix well. Spoon the mixture into a large strainer, pressing on the solids with the back of a spoon to drain any liquid. Reserve the filling.

3. Soak the corn husks in hot water to cover for 30 minutes, until the husks are soft and pliable. Separate the husks and rinse them under warm, running water.

4. Place the masa harina in a large mixing bowl. Add the oil, water, and salt and mix until smooth. When well blended, the masa should have the consistency of moist cookie dough. Add more water if needed.

5. Place a corn husk flat on a flat surface. With a rubber spatula, spread 2 tablespoons of masa in a thin layer across the husk and top with 2 tablespoons of the filling. Fold the sides of the husk one over the other, and then fold the top and bottom flaps in toward each other. Tie the flaps with a thin strip of corn husk. Repeat the procedure until the filling and masa are used.

6. Cook the tamales over simmering water for 1 to 1 1/4 hours, or until the masa is firm and doesn't stick to the corn husk. Unwrap one tamale to check its consistency.

7. Tamales are best eaten warm. You may serve them in the husks, or unwrapped with red or green chile sauce.

WORKING WITH CORN HUSKS

Tamales have been made in Mexico for centuries and were introduced here in New Mexico as a Christmas treat. Wrapping foods to be cooked in leaves or other vegetable products is one of the most ancient styles of food preparation. Corn husk wrappers have been common in countries where corn has played an important role in the people's diet.

Large ears of field corn provide the dried husks that are traditionally used to prepare tamales. Packages of husks can be found in the produce sections of Hispanic markets and supermarkets and through the Santa Fe School of Cooking mail order.

To dry fresh corn husks, carefully remove the husks from the corn cob by cutting with a sharp knife where the husks are attached and carefully peeling off the husks in layers. Place the husks on surfaces in direct sunlight and allow to dry naturally over a period of a few days until they turn pale yellow and become brittle. Stored in a sealed plastic bag, the husks will be usable for a year.

In addition to being used for tamales, the dried husks can be soaked and used to line a casserole dish for a creamy corn pudding, tamale pie, or squash casserole. The aroma of the cooked corn husks is fragrant, and the dishes take on a festive Southwestern air.

Sopa de Lima

Centerpiece **SOUPS**

Once prepared in large, micaceous clay pots over fires, soups have had a long tradition in Santa Fe and the Southwest. When the chill of autumn is in the air, simmering soups fill the homes of New Mexicans with comforting aromas. The soups found in this chapter are hearty and full of the flavors of the Southwest. With big, bold flavors, these satisfying and nourishing soups could be used to begin a meal or, paired with tortillas or bread, become a meal themselves.

Black Bean Soup

SERVES 6 TO 8

4 sprigs fresh rosemary or 1 teaspoon dried

6 sprigs fresh thyme or 1 teaspoon dried

6 sprigs fresh oregano or 2 teaspoons dried

1/4 ounce fresh epazote or 1 tablespoon dried (See p. 134)

1/4 cup canola or olive oil

3 to 4 dried chiles de arbol, chiles chipotles, or chiles moritas, or 2 teaspoons crushed red pepper

2 cups chopped white onion

2 teaspoons minced garlic

1 pound smoked pork shanks

2 teaspoons freshly ground toasted cumin seed

2 teaspoons freshly ground toasted coriander seed

1 teaspoon ground canela or 1/2 teaspoon ground cinnamon

1/8 teaspoon ground cloves or allspice

1 pound dried black turtle beans, picked over and soaked overnight in water to cover

8 to 10 cups chicken broth

2 to 3 teaspoons cider, red wine, or sherry vinegar

1 to 2 teaspoons coarse salt or to taste

1/4 cup finely diced red onion for garnish

1/2 cup sour cream for garnish

There are many beans which are indigenous to New Mexico, but not the black bean, which is from Central and South America. Black beans, also called turtle beans, have become very popular in Santa Fe because of their wonderful flavor. Chef Kathi Long developed this version of black bean soup as part of the Cuisines of Mexico class. Kathi has studied Mexican cuisine extensively and travels frequently in Mexico. She has worked with Patricia Quintana, author of *Feasts of Life* and *The Tastes of Mexico* (both from Council Oak Books).

1. Tie the fresh herbs and epazote into a bundle with kitchen string.
2. Heat the oil in a 6-quart pot over medium-high heat and sauté the chiles for 30 seconds or until toasted but not burned. Add the onions and garlic and sauté for 3 to 4 minutes, or until softened. Add the pork and the herb bundle, or dried herbs if using. Stir in the spices, beans, and 8 cups of the broth and combine well. Bring to a boil over medium-high heat. Reduce the heat and simmer, uncovered, stirring occasionally, for 2 to 3 hours or until the beans are soft.
3. Add the vinegar and salt and simmer the soup an additional 30 minutes. Remove the pork shanks, herb bundle, and chiles, if desired. Serve the soup in bowls and garnish with chopped red onion and a dollop of sour cream.

USING VINEGAR

The Spaniards brought sherry vinegar to Mexico, and the culinary inventiveness of the Mexican cooks brought it to the Mexican cuisine. Adding a small amount of vinegar when finishing bean soups or chile sauces rounds out and balances the flavors.

Green Chile Stew

SERVES 8

3 tablespoons
vegetable oil

1 1/2 pounds beef sirloin
or pork butt, cut in 1-inch
cubes

1 1/2 cups diced onion

1 tablespoon minced garlic

6 cups chicken or
beef broth

1 pound red or white
potatoes, cut in 1-inch
cubes

2 to 3 teaspoons salt, to
taste

3 cups roasted, peeled,
chopped green chiles

3 tablespoons diced red
bell pepper

2 tablespoons chopped
cilantro, or to taste

There are so many recipes and adaptations for green chile stew that it is impossible to list them all, and local cooks usually add what they have on hand. The following recipe consistently produces a rich, hearty stew. The piquancy of the stew depends upon the heat level of the chiles used, so choose the chiles that suit your taste. We use a tender cut of meat in classes due to the limited time frame. However, simmering a less-tender cut of meat prior to adding the vegetables will work perfectly well. This recipe is actually better when made a day ahead.

1. Heat the oil in a 6-quart pot over high heat and brown the meat in batches. Set aside.
2. In the same oil, sauté the onions until golden. Add the garlic and sauté 1 minute. Return the meat to the pan along with any juices that have accumulated.
3. Add the broth, potatoes, and salt and bring to a boil. Reduce the heat and simmer for 1 hour, until the potatoes are tender.
4. Add the green chiles and the red bell pepper, and cook 15 to 20 minutes more. Add the cilantro, stir, and serve.

GREEN CHILES

At the school we use locally grown green chiles when making this stew. We roast them over a fire or gas flame, peel them, and chop them. When the chile is not in season, we use roasted, peeled, chopped frozen green chiles. A combination of frozen mild and hot chiles produces a more balanced flavor.

Chicken Stock

YIELD: APPROXIMATELY 10 CUPS

14 cups water

4-5 pounds chicken bones (backs, wings, gizzards)

3 onions, quartered

1 large head of garlic, cut in half horizontally

4 large carrots, cut in small pieces

6 stalks celery, cut in small pieces

4 large bay leaves

6 sprigs each thyme, rosemary, marjoram

1 bunch Italian flat leaf or curly parsley

Salt to taste, optional

So many of the recipes at the Cooking School call for the use of chicken stock that there is hardly a day that stock is not cooking on the stove. As people wander through the School, the first thing they comment on is how wonderful the kitchen smells. Many of our recipes, such as posole, are dependent upon a good chicken stock. Following is the basic recipe we use.

1. Place the water and the bones in a large stockpot. Bring to a boil and then reduce the heat. Simmer for 1 hour.
2. Add the vegetables, bay leaves, herbs, and salt, and continue simmering for an additional 2 hours.
3. Strain out the bones, vegetables, and seasonings and cool the stock. Refrigerate overnight. Remove the fat, divide the stock into containers, and freeze for later use.

BROTH VERSUS STOCK

Broth and stock share common ingredients such as meat of some sort, onions, carrots, celery, and herbs to add flavor to the liquid, like thyme, bay leaves, or parsley.

Broth is made with whole meats and/or parts and simmered until the meat is just cooked. The meat is then removed from the liquid to be rejoined with the broth and vegetables in a soup or used separately in another preparation.

Stock, however is made from bones, pieces of meat, and vegetables which give the stock flavor, and it is simmered for 3 to 4 hours. Long-cooked stock will give you the very best results because the bones release their gelatin, giving the stock a lovely, rich consistency, and the meat, vegetables, and herbs will release their flavors.

TOASTING SPICES

The simplicity of the ingredients often belies the complexity of the flavors of New Mexican cuisine. The technique employed to intensify and deepen the flavors of spices is dry toasting. With exposure to heat, spices take on heightened flavors. To dry toast whole spices, heat a small skillet over medium-high heat for 1 minute. Add the whole seeds and stir until fragrant and their color has begun to deepen, taking care not to burn the seeds. Pour the toasted seeds onto another plate to cool. Place the seeds in a coffee grinder and finely grind the toasted seeds. Store in a tightly sealed container away from direct sunlight. Only toast as many seeds as you will use in a 5-day period and then repeat the procedure.

Caldo de Albondigas (Meatball Soup)

SERVES 8 TO 10

MEATBALLS:

1 pound lean ground beef or pork

1/4 cup diced onion, lightly browned in 1 tablespoon oil

2 teaspoons minced jalapeño

2 teaspoons chopped fresh cilantro

1 egg, lightly beaten

2 tablespoons fresh bread crumbs

1 teaspoon salt

SOUP:

Vegetable cooking spray

1 medium onion, diced

2 red bell peppers, diced

1 cup diced yellow squash

8 cups chicken stock

1 cup roasted, peeled, diced green chile

3 tablespoons minced canned chipotle chiles

1 teaspoon salt

1/4 cup coarsely chopped cilantro

1. In a stainless steel mixing bowl, combine all the meatball ingredients and mix well. Form into small meatballs and reserve.

2. Spray a medium skillet with vegetable cooking spray and sauté the onions, bell peppers, and squash for 5 minutes.

3. Add the stock, green chile, chipotle chiles, and salt. Bring to a boil, add the meatballs, and simmer the soup for 30 minutes. Add the fresh chopped cilantro near the end of the cooking time.

STORAGE OF CILANTRO

Because cilantro is a rather delicate herb, you want to choose bunches that are bright green with perfect leaves that are not yellow or wilted. The stems have as much flavor as the leaves, so all but the coarsest ones can be used. To store, re-cut the stem ends and place in 1/2-inch of water. Cover with a plastic bag to keep the cilantro fresh, and it will last for a week or more.

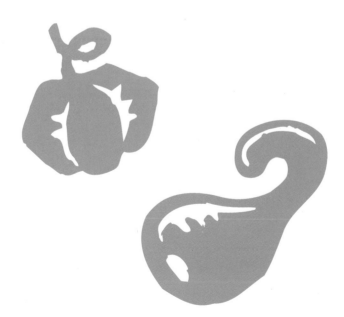

Tortilla Soup with Steak Ribbons

SERVES 6

1 tablespoon vegetable oil

1 onion, finely chopped

2 green bell peppers, finely chopped

8 cups chicken stock

1/2 cup fresh green chiles, diced

2 tablespoons Chimayo ground chile, mild or medium

1/3 cup cooked posole

1/3 cup cooked pinto beans

1/2 cup diced fresh tomato

1 tablespoon finely chopped fresh oregano

GARNISH:

Sprigs of fresh cilantro

2 corn tortillas, cut into 1/4-inch strips and fried crisp

6 thin strips of sirloin steak

6 bamboo skewers, soaked in water for 20 minutes

Tortilla Soup is a very popular Southwestern dish and one that cooks who come to the school often ask for.

1. Heat the oil in a large saucepan over medium-high heat and sauté the onion and bell peppers until browned around the edges.
2. Add the stock, chile, chile powder, posole, pinto beans, tomatoes, and oregano. Simmer for 30 minutes.
3. Thread steak strips onto the skewers and grill until cooked according to your taste.
4. Serve soup in large bowls and garnish with fresh cilantro, tortillas strips, and the skewered steak ribbons.

New Mexican Green Chile and Cabbage Soup with Sausage

SERVES 10 TO 12

8 tablespoons butter (1 stick)

1/2 green cabbage, shredded

10 ounces small new potatoes, unpeeled and cut into 1/2-inch cubes

1 medium onion, coarsely chopped

1 pound mushrooms, wiped clean and thinly sliced

8 tablespoons flour (1/2 cup)

8 cups chicken stock

1 cup roasted, peeled, diced green chiles

2 teaspoons salt

1 teaspoon freshly ground black pepper

2 teaspoons coarsely chopped fresh dill

1/2 pound smoked link sausage, cooked and diced

2 tablespoons coarsely chopped fresh cilantro

Chef Jeff Pufal developed this rich, hearty soup. It has become one of my favorite soups for a cold, wintry day.

1. Heat the butter in the bottom of a large pot over medium heat and sauté the cabbage, potatoes, onion, and mushrooms for 2 to 3 minutes.
2. Sprinkle the flour over all the ingredients and stir to combine thoroughly. Add the stock, green chiles, salt, pepper, and dill and simmer for 15 to 20 minutes.
3. Add the sausage and continue simmering for 5 minutes. Stir in the cilantro, and serve with croutons or fried tortilla strips.

POTATO VARIETIES

A variety of potatoes are grown in New Mexico and many are available at the Santa Fe Farmer's Market. In addition to the common russet and new potatoes, the farmers in New Mexico are growing some of the more rare varieties, including Fingerling, Russian Banana, Yukon Gold, Purple Peruvian, and Rose Finn Apple. Any of these types would be good in the New Mexico Green Chile and Cabbage Soup.

Savory and Cool Gazpacho

YIELD: 8 CUPS

1/2 cup coarsely chopped
red bell pepper

1/2 cup coarsely chopped
green bell pepper

1/2 cup coarsely chopped
yellow bell pepper

1 cup peeled, seeded,
and coarsely chopped
cucumber

1/2 cup coarsely chopped
celery

1/2 cup peeled and
coarsely chopped carrot

1/2 cup coarsely chopped
red onion

1/4 cup roasted, peeled,
seeded New Mexico
green chile

1 teaspoon minced garlic

2 cups tomato juice

2 cups V-8 Vegetable Juice

1 tablespoon fresh
lime juice

1 tablespoon sherry or red
wine vinegar

1 teaspoon Mexican
oregano

1 1/2 teaspoons salt,
or to taste

GARNISH:

3 tablespoons vegetable oil

3 corn tortillas, cut in
very thin strips

Sour cream (optional)

2 tablespoons coarsely
chopped fresh cilantro

Because Santa Fe has an elevation of 7,000 feet and is at the base of the Sangre de Cristo Mountains, it rarely gets above 90 degrees in the summer. There are days, however, when this cold soup is refreshingly welcome.

1. Place the bell peppers, cucumber, celery, carrot, red onion, green chile, and garlic in the work bowl of a food processor. Pulse the ingredients until finely chopped but not puréed. Pour this mixture into a large bowl and stir in the remaining gazpacho ingredients. Place the bowl in the refrigerator and chill for 1 to 2 hours.

2. Heat the oil in a small skillet over medium-high heat and fry the tortilla strips in two batches until crisp. Drain on paper towels.

3. Serve the gazpacho in chilled bowls garnished with a dollop of sour cream, a sprinkling of fresh cilantro, and fried tortilla strips.

OREGANO AND MARJORAM

In New Mexico, the herbs oregano and marjoram are often used interchangeably in food preparation. Aromatic, sweet, and mild in flavor, marjoram is considered best in its fresh form. Mexican oregano is more intensely flavored than is the Mediterranean oregano and is usually used dried.

BAKING VERSUS FRYING

This trick of baking, rather than frying, the tortilla strips creates a reduced fat, almost guilt-free chip. Preheat the oven to 400 degrees. Cut the tortillas in half and then crosswise into 1/4-inch strips. Place the strips on a baking sheet and spray lightly with a vegetable cooking spray. Turn and spray again. Bake about 8 minutes, or until golden and crisp. By cutting the tortillas into sixths, you can make tortilla chips in the same manner.

Heirloom Bean Stew with Chile, Corn, and Tomatoes

MAKES 12 CUPS

1 cup giant pinto, black runner, or Madeira beans, soaked overnight

3 tablespoons canola or olive oil

2 large onions, chopped

4 garlic cloves, minced

2 teaspoons toasted, ground cumin

1 tablespoon ground red chile

1 teaspoon Mexican oregano

2 quarts water

1 whole dried ancho or guajillo chile

Salt

4 large tomatoes, peeled, seeded, and chopped into large pieces

Kernels from 5 ears of corn (about 3 1/2 cups)

12 ounces summer squash, cut in large cubes

1/2 cup coarsely chopped fresh cilantro

Deborah Madison, who lives in Santa Fe and has taught several classes at the School, contributed this recipe. She is the author of *The Savory Way* (Bantam, 1990) and *The Greens Cookbook* (Bantam, 1987) and is currently working on a comprehensive vegetarian cookbook.

1. Drain the beans. Cover with fresh water, bring to a boil, and cook 10 minutes. Drain again and set aside.
2. In a large, heavy pot, heat the oil, add the onions, and sauté over medium heat, stirring frequently, until well browned. Add the garlic, cumin, ground chile, and oregano, cook together a few minutes, and then add the beans, 2 quarts water, and whole chile. Bring to a boil and simmer, partially covered, until the beans are soft, 1 to 1 1/2 hours.
3. Add 2 teaspoons salt, the tomatoes, corn, squash, and half the cilantro. Cook until the vegetables are tender. Add the remaining cilantro just before serving.

HEIRLOOM BEANS

Heirloom beans, such as tepary, bollito, and Anasazi, are domesticated wild beans which have been grown for centuries in Native American and Hispanic communities. There has been a revival of interest in recent years. This is due both to a concern for nutrition and an interest in preserving traditional foods and ways of life. Organizations such as Native Seed Search, Seed of Change, and Seed Savers Exchange have been instrumental in the survival and revival of indigenous crops. (See supplier information on page 173).

Heirloom Bean Stew

Sopa de Lima

YIELD: 6 SERVINGS

1 pound boneless, skinless chicken breasts

1 cup diced plum tomatoes

3/4 cup finely diced white or red onion

2 to 3 fresh serrano chiles, minced

1 medium-sized ripe Haas avocado, peeled, quartered, with seed removed (See Ripening Avocados, p. 30)

1/4 cup coarsely chopped fresh cilantro

6 cups chicken broth, heated

1/4 cup freshly squeezed lime juice, or to taste

2 teaspoons coarse salt, or to taste

This soup is a light, flavorful way to begin a summer supper. It gets its name from the "lima," a variety of lime that has a unique bergamot flavor and aroma and is indigenous to Mexico.

1. Place the chicken, with water to cover, in a saucepan over high heat and bring to a boil. Reduce the heat and simmer the chicken for 10 minutes, until cooked through. Turn off the heat and let the chicken cool in the broth. Shred the cooled chicken and set aside.
2. Divide the shredded chicken, tomatoes, onion, chiles, avocado, and cilantro among 6 large soup bowls. Pour the heated chicken broth into each bowl and season with lime juice and salt to taste. Serve immediately.

SELECTING TOMATOES

The favored variety of tomato for all-around use at the Cooking School is the pear-shaped Roma, also called Italian or plum. It has less juice and fewer seeds than other varieties of tomatoes. The Roma tomato should be stored at room temperature to maintain the tomato flavor and should not be refrigerated unless you are trying to prevent further ripening. Refrigeration inhibits the flavor of tomatoes and therefore should not be used unless absolutely necessary.

Wild Mint and Lamb Soup

SERVES 6

1 pound lamb stew meat, cut into 1-inch cubes

1 teaspoon salt

1/2 teaspoon black pepper

1 tablespoon olive oil

1 cup diced carrots

1 cup diced celery

2 tablespoons chopped mint leaves (fresh or dried)

4 cups water

4 cups lamb stock (recipe follows)

Wild mint leaves for garnish

LAMB STOCK:

5 pounds lamb shank bones or lamb loin bones

1 tablespoon olive oil

5 ripe tomatoes, quartered

2 leeks, coarsely chopped

5 celery stalks, coarsely chopped

4 large carrots, coarsely chopped

6 quarts water

4 bay leaves

1 bunch fresh parsley

2 bunches fresh thyme

2 bunches fresh rosemary

Lois Ellen Frank, Santa Fe resident and author of *Native American Cooking: Foods of the Southwest Indian Nations* contributed this recipe. Lois, a guest chef at the School of Cooking, is part Kiowa Indian and has spent years visiting Native American reservations and documenting techniques and recipes.*

1. Season the lamb with salt and pepper.
2. In a skillet, heat the olive oil over medium-high heat and add the meat. Brown the lamb for 3 minutes on each side until the lamb is medium-rare. Remove the meat from the pan and set aside.
3. Pour the water into a large pot, add the vegetables from the pan, and bring to a boil over high heat. Reduce the heat and simmer 10 minutes. Add the meat and bring to a boil once again over high heat.
4. Garnish with wild mint leaves and serve hot with one of the traditional Indian breads.

1. Preheat the oven to 450 degrees. Put the bones in a large roasting pan and brown in the oven about 1 hour, turning them every 20 minutes. Remove them from the oven and set aside.
2. In a large stock pot heat the olive oil, add the tomatoes, leeks, celery, and carrots, and sauté over high heat 15 minutes, stirring constantly. Add the bones, water, and herbs and bring to a boil over medium-high heat. Reduce the heat and simmer 4 1/2 to 5 hours, skimming the surface every half hour.
3. Remove from the heat and pour the stock through a sieve lined with cheesecloth. Discard the contents of the sieve.
4. Refrigerate the stock 3 hours, then remove the solidified fat from the top. The stock will keep 5 days in a covered container in the refrigerator or for several months in the freezer.

*This recipes appears in *Native American Cooking: Foods of the Southwest Indian Nations* (Clarkson, Potter, 1991).

LAMB IN NEW MEXICO

The presence of lamb in New Mexico dates back to the latter part of the sixteenth century with the arrival of the Spanish explorers. In 1540, Coronado brought 5,000 churro sheep to New Mexico. Today, rare breeds of sheep are still available through a livestock cooperative called Ganandos del Valley, whose goal is to preserve the traditions of raising sheep the natural way in northern New Mexico. Sheep graze on the mountain meadows of the Sangre de Cristo mountains during the summer months, which results in a naturally lean meat. Varieties of sheep raised include Churro, valued for its unique flavor, Karakul, and Poquitero. The lamb is occasionally available at the Santa Fe Farmer's Market. Whole and half lambs are available by calling Pastores Lamb (see supplier list on page 173) or by stopping by the Pastores Feed and General Store in the historic village of Los Ojos, which is located two hours north of Santa Fe in the high country. The drive to Los Ojos is well worth taking, and a visit to Tierra Wools, where wool from the sheep cooperative is spun and woven, is a must.

Santa Fe Fiesta Coleslaw

SALADS *That Sing*

Our selection of flavorful salad combinations offers an abundance of color, taste, and texture. Included are the typical leafy green salads as well as crunchy coleslaw and a wild rice and pasta salad. Salads offer a light touch to compliment the robust and spicy entrees of the Southwest. Recipes such as the Santa Fe Fiesta Coleslaw and the Jicama Watercress Salad use lighter dressings that reflect the many requests we get at the School for a healthful approach to cooking.

Avocado and Tomato Salad with Avocado Dressing

YIELD: 6 SERVINGS

DRESSING:

3 Haas avocados

1/3 cup coarsely chopped fresh cilantro

1/3 cup chopped white onion

1/2 to 3/4 cup water

1 tablespoon fresh lime juice

1 tablespoon cider vinegar

1 to 2 teaspoons coarse salt, or to taste

SALAD:

2 heads Romaine lettuce, outer leaves reserved for another use, inner leaves separated, rinsed, and thoroughly dried

2 bunches watercress, large stems removed

6 ripe plum tomatoes, cored and quartered

Pickled Red Onions (see page 115 for recipe), for garnish

1. Peel one avocado and cut into large cubes. Put the avocado cubes, cilantro, onion, water, lime juice, vinegar, and salt into a blender and purée until smooth. Refrigerate, covered with plastic wrap pressed against the surface of the dressing, until ready to use.

2. Cut the remaining avocados into quarters. Peel them and slice each quarter into thirds. (Each serving should include 4 slices of avocado.)

3. Arrange the Romaine hearts, watercress, tomatoes, and avocado slices on 6 salad plates. Garnish with Pickled Red Onions. Pass the avocado dressing separately.

Santa Fe Fiesta Coleslaw

YIELD: 6 SERVINGS

SLAW:

1 pound green cabbage, shredded

1 medium cucumber, peeled, seeded, and cut in thin, diagonal slices

5 scallions, thinly sliced on the diagonal

1 medium red bell pepper, cut into thin strips

1 medium yellow bell pepper, cut into thin strips

2 celery ribs, thinly sliced on the diagonal

1 large carrot, peeled and shredded

1 small white onion, peeled and cut into thin slivers (optional)

DRESSING:

1/4 cup freshly squeezed lime juice

2 tablespoons cider vinegar

1 teaspoon to 1 tablespoon hot pepper sauce, to taste

1/4 cup sugar

1 teaspoon salt

If you like your coleslaw tart-sweet, without mayonnaise, then this is the one for you. Fresh vegetables, tangy dressing, and no oil—what a great taste combination.

1. In a large mixing bowl, combine the cabbage, cucumber, scallions, bell peppers, celery, carrot, and onion.

2. In a small bowl combine the remaining ingredients and stir until the sugar has dissolved. Pour the dressing over the vegetables and toss well. Let the mixture stand at room temperature for at least 30 minutes, tossing often, before serving. For maximum color and flavor, serve within 3 to 4 hours.

Jicama Salad with Watercress, Radishes, and Chiles

WHAT IS JICAMA?

This crisply textured, slightly sweet, edible tuber resembling a brown-skinned turnip is sometimes called Mexican potatoe. The flavor of its white flesh is compared to that of a water chestnut or sweet radish, and it is usually eaten raw. Jicama is generally available in supermarkets year round. When buying, choose the smaller, young jicamas as they will be sweeter, and less starchy or woody, than the older, larger ones that can weigh a pound or more. Firm and unshriveled jicamas will keep, unwrapped, several weeks in the refrigerator. Sticks of peeled jicama, dipped in a little salt and hot chile powder and squirted with lime, make a terrific, low calorie snack.

YIELD: 6 SERVINGS

2 medium jicama, about 1 1/2 to 2 pounds, peeled, sliced 1/4-inch-thick, and cut into 1/4-inch-thick sticks

1 cup slivered red onion

1 1/3 cups julienned radishes

3 to 5 jalapeños, stemmed, seeded, ribbed, and thinly sliced lengthwise

2 bunches watercress, large stems removed

1/3 cup coarsely chopped fresh cilantro

1/2 cup freshly squeezed lime juice

1 tablespoon cider vinegar

2 tablespoons sugar

1 teaspoon salt or to taste

1. In a large bowl gently toss the jicama, red onion, radishes, chiles, watercress, and cilantro. Refrigerate until ready to use.

2. In a small bowl whisk together the lime juice, vinegar, sugar, and salt until the sugar is dissolved. Pour dressing over salad and toss to coat thoroughly. Adjust seasonings and serve immediately.

Red Chile Caesar Salad

Traditonal Caesar salad originated in Tijuana, Mexico. This version, developed by Bill Weiland, has a definite bite to it.

YIELD: 6 SERVINGS

Inner leaves of 3 to 4 heads of red or green Romaine lettuce, or a combination of both

1 cup Red Chile Caesar Dressing

Chile-Garlic Croutons

1/3 cup shaved parmesan cheese (See Note)

1. Place all ingredients except for the vinegar, chile, and oil in a food processor.
2. Place the vinegar and chile in an enamel or stainless steel saucepan and simmer for 3 minutes.
3. While the food processor is running, pour the vinegar mixture into the ingredients and slowly add all the oil. Refrigerate until ready to use.

RED CHILE CAESAR DRESSING:

YIELD: ABOUT 2 CUPS

1 tablespoon roasted garlic (See Roasting Garlic)

1 teaspoon salt

1 1/2 teaspoons dry mustard

6 anchovy fillets

1 teaspoon Worcestershire sauce

2 coddled eggs

2 tablespoons freshly squeezed lemon juice

1/4 cup grated parmesan cheese

1/3 cup red wine vinegar

2 to 3 tablespoons medium Chimayo ground red chile

1 cup olive oil

CHILE-GARLIC CROUTONS:

3 cloves fresh garlic, minced

1/3 cup olive oil

10 to 12 slices good French or Italian bread, sliced 1/2 inch thick and cut into 1/2-inch cubes

2 teaspoons mild ground Chimayo red chile

Salt to taste

1. Preheat the oven to 350 degrees.
2. In a small bowl mix together the garlic and the olive oil.
3. Place the bread cubes in a medium bowl and drizzle the garlic-oil mixture over the bread. Toss to combine well.
4. Sprinkle the ground red chile and the salt over the bread cubes and toss to thoroughly coat.
5. Spread the seasoned croutons on a baking sheet and bake for about 10 minutes, or until crisp and golden.

NOTE:

Shaving small sheets of parmesan cheese is much more attractive as a garnish for Caesar salad than sprinkling on the grated variety. Using a whole piece of parmesan, shave inch-wide pieces of cheese from the piece with a vegetable peeler. Refrigerate until ready to use.

ASSEMBLY:

1. Place the romaine leaves in a large bowl and add the dressing. Toss well.
2. Arrange the leaves on individual serving plates. Sprinkle with Chile-Garlic Croutons and top with shavings of parmesan cheese. Serve.

Seasonal Greens with Orange-Sherry Vinaigrette

YIELD: 6 SERVINGS

4 cups mixed greens, washed and thoroughly dried

1 small red onion, thinly sliced

2 small seedless oranges, skin removed and sliced into rounds

1/2 cup spiced or toasted pecans, chopped

Orange Sherry Vinaigrette

Salt and freshly ground black pepper to taste

1. Toss the greens with the red onion, orange, spiced pecans, and vinaigrette.
2. Season with salt and pepper and serve immediately.

ORANGE SHERRY VINAIGRETTE:

1/4 cup orange juice concentrate

2 tablespoons sherry vinegar

1/4 cup olive oil

Salt and freshly ground pepper to taste

1. Place the orange juice and sherry vinegar in a small bowl. Whisk in the olive oil and season with salt and pepper to taste.

ROASTING GARLIC

Preheat the oven to 350 degress. Cut the top third from whole heads of garlic. You may save these pieces of garlic from the top part for soups and stews, or you can roast them along with the larger portions. Sprinkle the cut surfaces with olive oil, salt, and pepper and wrap the heads in aluminum foil. Place the foil package in the oven and bake for 1 hour, until the cloves have softened and are golden. Let the garlic cool slightly. To remove the cloves, take a head, root end in the palm of your hand, and squeeze. The carmelized cloves will emerge and you can use them as you wish. Keep them refrigerated and they will be usable for 8 to 10 days.

MIXED GREENS

During the summer at the Santa Fe Farmers' Market, you will find wonderful combinations of soft greens and lettuces such as amaranth, arugula, Belgian endive, chicory (frisee), garden cresses, dandelion, romaine and looseleaf lettuces (red and green leaf), butter (Boston) lettuce, mache (lamb's lettuce), mizuna, baby red mustard greens, radicchio, sorrel, spinach, wild spinach, and tatsoi. These greens provide an exciting range of textures and flavors. Greens have a high water content, so they wilt easily. Buy the freshest, greenest leaves, avoiding those that are yellow or faded. Store them unwashed in the refrigerator wrapped in damp paper towels inside a plastic bag punctured in several places to allow air flow. Greens are low in calories and most are high in potassium, calcium, and vitamin A.

Southwestern Salad

Janet Mitchell is credited with this terrific salad of spices, chopped vegetables, grains, and pasta. It makes a delicious accompaniment for grilled entrees, meats, or a vegetarian buffet. It is low in calories and fat, and high in complex carbohydrates, fiber, and protein.

1. Mix all salad ingredients together. In a small bowl, whisk all vinaigrette ingredients together.
2. Pour vinaigrette over salad ingredients and combine well. Let the mixture set at room temperature for 1 hour before serving.

YIELD: 18 SERVINGS

SALAD:

4 cups cooked black beans, or two 15-ounce cans, rinsed and drained

1 cup cooked wild rice

2 cups frozen corn, thawed

2 cups cooked orzo

1/2 cup diced red pepper

1/2 cup chopped red onion

3 fresh jalapeño chiles, seeded and minced

1/2 cup chopped fresh cilantro

VINAIGRETTE:

1/2 cup red wine vinegar

1/2 cup olive oil

2 tablespoons lime juice

1 teaspoon toasted ground cumin seed

1 teaspoon salt, or to taste

ALL ABOUT OLIVE OIL

Due in large part to the health consciousness of America, sales of olive oil have been steadily growing. It is one of the top three best-selling oils in the country. It is hard to match the rich, complex aroma of the extra-virgin oil from Italy, France, Spain, and Greece. However, California has added its name to the list and has produced some wonderful examples.

To qualify as extra virgin, olive oil must contain less than 1 percent acidity. To qualify as virgin oil, it must contain less than 2 percent acidity. Pure olive oil is refined from the pulp remaining from earlier pressings which are pressed again with ground skins and olive pits. This grade is the least flavorful because refining leaves the oil virtually tasteless. Sometimes, a percentage of extra virgin or virgin oil is added to revive the color and taste. Oils processed by the cold-press method are superior and can be purchased in specialty and natural foods markets.

The health benefits of olive oil are many. Nearly 3/4 of its fat content is monounsaturated, which lowers "bad" cholesterol (LDL) while leaving the "good" cholesterol (HDL) intact. It also contains vitamin E and other antioxidants that are considered anti-carcinogenic.

Lime Marinated Grilled Salmon

Memorable
MAIN COURSES

The focus of each Cooking School class is defined by the main course, which varies from traditional dishes to more contemporary recipes, including vegetarian meals and lighter cuisine. Some of the "old standby" recipes such as enchiladas and carne adovada have warmed the souls and stomachs of New Mexicans for years, while more modern recipes combine the hearty flavors of red and green chiles with other ingredients such as citrus and tropical fruits to produce unforgettable flavors.

Birria

YIELD: 6 TO 8 SERVINGS

3 to 4 pounds beef brisket

2 tablespoons vegetable oil

1 cup chopped onion

6 cloves garlic, chopped

2 cups roasted, peeled, seeded, and chopped New Mexican green chiles

3 teaspoons dried Mexican oregano

2 cups peeled and chopped tomatoes, fresh or canned

2 cups beef broth or water

Salt to taste

Janet Mitchell developed this flavorful version of birria, or beef simmered with onions, tomatoes, and chiles. Birria is popular in the northern Mexican state of Sonora, which has a reputation in Mexico as the land of good beef. There are accounts of birria being one of the dishes enjoyed by the Mexicans as they celebrated their independence from Spain in 1821. Although somewhat time consuming, the hand shredding of the meat is important to the texture and character of this dish. Birria can be served as an entree, a filling for burritos or tacos, or as a stuffing for sopaipillas. Avoid using mediocre fresh tomatoes in this dish. If no really good fresh tomatoes are available, use high-quality canned ones instead.

1. Preheat the oven to 325 degrees.
2. Brown the beef in the oil and remove from the pan. Add the onion and garlic to the oil and sauté until soft.
3. Place all ingredients in a roasting pan. Cover and bake for 3 hours, or until the meat is very tender and starts to fall apart. Turn the meat occasionally, adding broth or water if the mixture seems dry.
4. Remove the meat, allow to cool enough to handle, and then shred with your fingers, discarding any fat or connective tissue. Place roasting pan on the cooktop and simmer until the remaining liquid is reduced to about 2 cups. Mix shredded meat with the sauce.

Black and Red Pork Tenderloin

YIELD: 6 SERVINGS

1/2 cup pure ground Chimayo red chile, medium

1/4 cup freshly ground black pepper

2 pounds pork tenderloin, trimmed

2 tablespoons butter

2 tablespoons canola or vegetable oil

2 cups Onion and Chile Madeira Cream Sauce (see page 114 for recipe)

Chef Jeff Pufal created this dish as part of our Contemporary Southwest III class and it immediately became one of our favorite dishes. You may decrease the amount of chile in the rub if you find this too spicy for your tastes or if the chile seems particularly hot.

1. Preheat the oven to 350 degrees.
2. Combine the red chile and the black pepper and spread the mixture on a baking sheet. Roll the pork in the mixture, pressing the spices onto the pork. Chill for at least 30 minutes.
3. Heat the butter and oil in a medium skillet over medium-high heat. Sear the pork on all sides and remove to a baking sheet. Bake 10 to 15 minutes, until the pork is still moist and not dried out. Let the tenderloins rest for 5 minutes and slice in 1/4-inch slices. Serve with Onion and Chile Madeira Cream Sauce.

Carne Adovada

YIELD: 8 SERVINGS

1/3 cup peanut or vegetable oil

3 1/2 pounds pork loin or butt, cut in 3/4-inch cubes

2 cups diced onion

2 tablespoons minced garlic

4 cups chicken broth or water, divided

1 teaspoon ground canela

2 teaspoons ground cumin seed

2 teaspoons ground coriander seed

2 teaspoons dried Mexican oregano

2 teaspoons chile caribe (crushed red chile pods)

3/4 cup Chimayo ground red chile, mild or medium

1 tablespoon Red Chile Honey (See page 131)

2 tablespoons sherry vinegar or red wine vinegar

1 to 2 teaspoons salt, to taste

Carne adovada is one of the spiciest and most popular dishes we serve at the School. Over the years, the recipe has been adapted to make the dish more flavorful and tender. It reheats wonderfully and is actually better the day after it is made.

1. Preheat the oven to 350 degrees.
2. Heat the oil in a large skillet and brown the pork in batches. Set the pork aside. Add the onions to the skillet and sauté until golden. Add the garlic and sauté for 1 minute. Deglaze the skillet with 1 cup of the chicken broth, loosening the browned bits by rubbing the pan with the back of a spoon.
3. Place the canela, cumin, coriander, oregano, chile caribe, red chile, honey, vinegar, and salt in the workbowl of a food processor. Add the cooked onions, garlic, and broth from the skillet and 2 more cups of chicken broth to the processor and run the machine until the mixture is thoroughly combined.
4. Place the browned pork, the chile marinade, and the remaining 1 cup chicken broth in an oven-proof pot or dish, stir to combine well, and bake for 1 hour or until the pork is tender. Serve the carne adovada over chile rellenos, over rice, wrapped in a flour tortilla as a burrito, or with beans and posole.

VARIATION:

The traditional method for making this dish is to eliminate step 2 and mix the marinade ingredients with the raw onions and garlic. Pour this over the unbrowned meat. Cover the mixture and refrigerate overnight. Pour the meat and the marinade into an ovenproof casserole or pot and bake, covered, for 2 to 2 1/2 hours, or until tender. The method described at left, although not traditional, brings out the flavors of the onion, garlic, and pork because the ingredients are browned first. Whichever method you choose, the dish is full of flavor and will be a favorite.

Cheese Enchiladas for a Crowd

YIELD: 10 SERVINGS

3 cups Red Chile Sauce (see page 118 for the recipe)

16 fresh corn tortillas, about 4 inches in diameter

1 1/2 pounds cheddar cheese, grated

1 1/2 cups diced onion, or sliced scallions with green tops

2 cups shredded iceberg or romaine lettuce

1 1/2 cups diced tomato

1 1/4 cups sour cream

Enchiladas are probably the most popular dish served in New Mexican restaurants. They are on every menu. This recipe was one of the very first ones used at the Santa Fe School of Cooking. We have prepared this recipe so many times that you would think we would tire of it, but the aroma of the enchilada casserole is still mouth-watering. Traditionally, in New Mexico enchiladas are stacked rather than rolled, which is a much easier way to fix them and makes them a great choice for large dinner parties.

1. Preheat the oven to 350 degrees. Oil a 9 x 12-inch baking dish or pan.
2. Spread about 1 cup of the sauce over the bottom of the dish and layer half of the tortillas evenly over the sauce. Top the tortillas with a third of the cheese and sprinkle with half the onion. If you prefer a milder onion flavor, use the scallions. Repeat to make a second layer and top with the last cup of sauce and the remaining cheese. Bake 20 to 30 minutes, until bubbly (heated through) and lightly browned.
3. To serve, spoon portions onto dinner plates, garnish with finely shredded lettuce and diced tomato, and top with 2 tablespoons of the sour cream. Serve with pinto beans and posole.

VARIATION:

Rolled enchiladas are served in most parts of the United States and Mexico. If you would like to roll your enchiladas, you must first soften them. Pour 1/2 inch of oil in a skillet and heat until the surface ripples, but do not let the oil smoke. With tongs, dip each tortilla into the hot oil momentarily. Remove the tortilla from the oil and place on paper towels. If you leave the tortilla in the hot oil for too long it will become too crisp to roll. Place several tablespoons of the filling down the center of the tortillas, roll them tightly, and place them, seam side down and side by side, in a shallow baking dish. Top with sauce and bake at 350 degrees for 20 minutes, or until the cheese is melted.

Basic Chicken Enchiladas

YIELD: 10 SERVINGS

3 cups Green Chile Sauce (see page 111 for the recipe)

16 fresh corn tortillas, about 4 inches in diameter

4 cups cooked shredded chicken

1 1/2 pounds Monterey Jack cheese, grated

1 1/2 cups diced onion, or sliced scallions with green tops

2 cups shredded iceberg or romaine lettuce

1 1/2 cups diced tomato

1 1/4 cups sour cream

The quality of an enchilada is highly dependent upon the flavor of the chile sauce. Personal preferences for either red or green chile sauce run deep in Santa Fe. If you are undecided, order your dish served with half red and half green, which is done in Santa Fe by ordering "Christmas." Any waitperson will know what you are requesting. However, one visitor became a little confused and ordered enchiladas "Santa Claus style." At the Cooking School, we encourage visitors to try both the red and green sauces so they can experience the differences in flavors.

1. Preheat the oven to 350 degrees. Oil a 9 x 12-inch baking dish or pan.
2. Spread about 1 cup of the sauce over the bottom of the dish and layer half of the tortillas evenly over the sauce. Top the tortillas with half the chicken and a third of the cheese and sprinkle with half the onion. If you prefer a milder onion flavor, use the scallions. Repeat to make a second layer and top with the last cup of sauce and the remaining cheese. Bake 20 to 30 minutes, until bubbly and lightly browned.
3. To serve, spoon portions onto dinner plates, garnish with finely shredded lettuce and diced tomato, and top with 2 tablespoons of the sour cream. Serve with pinto beans and posole.

SERVING CHICKEN ENCHILADAS

A sunny-side-up fried egg is frequently served with enchiladas. The egg seems to round out the flavors of the chile, cheese, and onion and cuts the heat if the chiles are particularly hot.

Chilaquiles with Chicken and Green Chile-Tomatillo Sauce

This recipe for chilaquiles is part of our Southwest Breakfast class, as chilaquiles are generally eaten at breakfast or brunch, frequently accompanying eggs or meats. They are traditionally made by briefly cooking fried tortilla wedges in a simmering sauce. They may also be enriched with grated cheese, cream, and/or cooked meat.

YIELD: 6 TO 8 SERVINGS

1 dozen corn tortillas

Canola oil or vegetable oil for frying

3 1/2 cups Green Chile-Tomatillo Sauce

1 1/2 cups cooked, shredded chicken

1 small onion, cut in slivers

2 cups grated Monterey Jack cheese

Sour cream for garnish

1. Preheat the oven to 350 degrees.
2. Cut the tortillas into sixths. Heat 1/2 inch of oil in a skillet over medium heat. Fry the tortilla wedges, in batches if necessary, until golden. Drain on paper towels.
3. Lightly oil a 9 x 12-inch baking dish. Layer one-third of the chips on the bottom of the dish. Sprinkle a layer of sauce over the chips with consecutive layers of chicken, onion, and cheese. Add another third of the chips with sauce, chicken, onion, and cheese. Top with the remaining layer of chips with sauce and cheese. Bake until golden and bubbly. Serve with sour cream.

GREEN CHILE-TOMATILLO SAUCE:

2 tablespoons vegetable oil

1/3 cup finely chopped onion

2 tablespoons minced garlic

1 1/2 cups husked, rinsed, quartered fresh tomatillos, or canned, drained

1 1/2 cups roasted, chopped green chile, hot or mild

1/2 cup thinly sliced green onions

3/4 cup chicken broth

1/2 cup heavy cream

1 teaspoon salt, or to taste

Fresh lime juice, to taste

1. Heat the oil in a medium saucepan over medium-high heat and sauté the onion for 2 minutes. Add the garlic and cook for 2 minutes more, stirring occasionally.
2. Place the tomatillos in the workbowl of a food processor and pulse until the tomatillos are finely chopped. Add the tomatillos, chile, green onions, chicken broth, and cream to the saucepan, bring to a boil, and lower the heat so the sauce is barely simmering. Cook for about 40 minutes. Season to taste with salt and lime juice.

Chiles Rellenos

YIELD: 6 SERVINGS

This recipe has been taught at the Cooking School for many years in the Traditional New Mexican II class. Deep frying rellenos requires that they be served immediately or they become soggy. I would not recommend making this recipe for large dinner parties as it is labor intensive, but rather for a small group.

1. Roast the chiles over a flame until charred and place in a plastic bag to sweat for 15 to 20 minutes. Keeping the stems intact, carefully peel the chiles. With the tip of a small knife, make a slit in the chiles the length of each pod. Remove the seeds. Rinse under cool, running water and drain on paper towels.
2. Mix the cheeses and oregano in a small bowl. Stuff the cheese mixture into each of the chiles and press the opening closed. Place the chiles on a tray covered with a layer of paper towels and refrigerate for at least 1

WHAT DOES THE BEER DO?

The primary purpose of the beer is to lighten and leaven the batter, although the beer does impart a mild flavor. If you prefer, seltzer water can be substituted for the beer in the chiles rellenos batter recipe.

12 small fresh New Mexican green chiles or Poblano chiles

1 3/4 cups grated Monterey Jack cheese

1/2 cup grated cheddar cheese

2 teaspoons dried Mexican oregano

Canola oil for frying

6 eggs, separated

2/3 cup beer, preferably New Mexican or Mexican

1 3/4 cups flour

2 teaspoons pure ground medium Chimayo red chile

1/2 to 3/4 teaspoon salt, to taste

2 cups Red Chile Sauce (optional)

1/2 cup sour cream

hour to overnight to allow the stuffing to chill.

3. When you are ready to prepare the batter, heat the canola oil in a deep pot or deep fat fryer to 375 degrees.

4. Beat the egg whites until they hold soft peaks. In another bowl, whisk the egg yolks, beer, flour, red chile, and salt together until smooth. Fold in the egg whites.

5. Remove the stuffed chiles from the refrigerator. Dip one chile into the batter, coating thoroughly, and carefully place in the hot oil. Repeat with 1 to 2 more chiles, frying each to a golden brown, about 4 to 5 minutes. Remove from oil and drain on paper towels. Repeat with remaining chiles.

6. Serve two chile rellenos per person. Top with Red Chile Sauce and sour cream.

VARIATIONS:

Should you want to make them ahead, or if you prefer a lower-calorie dish, you can bake rather than deep-fry the rellenos. To make this a casserole, prepare the stuffed chiles and batter as described above, and preheat the oven to 400 degrees. Oil a shallow rectangular baking pan which will just hold the stuffed chiles side by side. Spread half the batter in the baking pan, lay the chiles in a single layer over the batter, and cover them with the remaining batter. Bake for about 15 minutes, or until puffed and brown on top. You can also sprinkle with a little more cheese and place it under the broiler for a minute or so to lightly brown.

For a more contemporary taste, try filling these chiles with one of the following:

A mix of sautéed vegetables, such as cubed zucchini, chayote, and fresh corn

• Cooked black beans and shrimp sautéed with onion and garlic

• Refried beans with cheese

• Shredded chicken and green onion

• Piccadillo (ground beef seasoned with cumin, coriander, canela, Mexican oregano, currants, and toasted pine nuts)

WORKING WITH FRAGILE CHILES

Sometimes chiles can fall apart as you dip them into the batter before frying. Should you be working with chiles that are exceptionally fragile, use this technique: heat a good 2 inches of oil in a medium-size skillet to 375 degrees. Drop ovals of batter that approximate chile shapes onto the hot oil, place a stuffed chile on each oval, and cover with more batter. Fry until golden brown, about 3 minutes, on both sides.

Chile-Marinated Pork Tenderloin with Roasted Pineapple Salsa

YIELD: 6 TO 8 SERVINGS

CHILE MARINADE:

1 tablespoon ground ancho chile

2 tablespoons ground Chimayo chile

2 tablespoons minced white onion

3 teaspoons minced garlic

1/3 cup chopped fresh cilantro

2 tablespoons chopped fresh oregano, or
1 tablespoon dried Mexican oregano

1 teaspoon freshly ground cumin seed

1/3 cup freshly squeezed lime or lemon juice

1/3 cup fruity olive oil

Salt to taste

1. Mix all ingredients in a small bowl, combine well, and reserve.

PORK LOIN:

2 pounds boneless pork loin, sliced 1/2-inch thick

ROASTED PINEAPPLE SALSA:

1 medium-sized pineapple, peeled and sliced 1/4-inch thick

1/2 cup minced red onion

1 cup chopped fresh cilantro

1 jalapeño chile, seeded and minced

2 tablespoons rice wine vinegar

1/2 teaspoon hot-pepper sauce, or to taste

Salt to taste

1. Place sliced pork loin in a large plastic bag. Add the marinade and coat the meat thoroughly. Seal the bag and refrigerate for 1 hour at room temperature or 4 hours refrigerated. Return the pork to room temperature before cooking.

1. Grill pineapple slices until lightly browned on both sides.
2. Cool, remove pineapple cores, and dice.
3. Combine all ingredients and season to taste with salt. Cover and allow to sit at room temperature for 1 hour. The salsa is best if mixed 1 hour before serving. However, the ingredients can be prepared several hours in advance and combined just prior to serving.

ASSEMBLY:

1. Preheat a grill or broiler. Lightly brush the grill rack with vegetable oil.
2. Remove slices of pork loin from the marinade, brushing off the excess marinade by hand. Grill the slices on each side until cooked through but still juicy inside, about 3 to 4 minutes per side.
3. To serve, top the grilled pork loin slices with several spoonfuls of pineapple salsa.

Oven Roasted Cornish Game Hens, Santa Fe Style

YIELD: 6 SERVINGS

3 20-ounce Cornish game hens

2 to 3 tablespoons vegetable oil or butter

1 tablespoon pure ground Chimayo chile

Salt to taste

Chef Bill Weiland developed this spicy version of a classic dish for our Southwest Cooking II class. The cornish game hen is served with a Southwestern adaptation of polenta (see page 137 for the recipe) and Green Chile Chasseur Sauce (see page 110 for the recipe). If using 20-ounce Cornish game hens, they may be split to serve two guests each.

1. Preheat the oven to 375 degrees.
2. Split the hens in half, cutting through the breast bone. Spread open the hens and cut out the back bone by cutting through the rib bones on either side. Place the halves on a sheet pan skin side up. Brush the hens with the vegetable oil and sprinkle with chile and salt. Bake 20 to 30 minutes, until cooked through.

Grilled Shrimp in Achiote Marinade

YIELD: 6 SERVINGS

ACHIOTE MARINADE:

3 tablespoons olive oil

4 large garlic cloves, peeled

3 3.5-ounce packages Achiote Condimentado, crumbled

4 tablespoons frozen orange juice concentrate

1/3 cup fresh grapefruit juice

2 tablespoons cider vinegar

1/4 cup water

1 teaspoon freshly ground cumin seed

2 teaspoons freshly ground coriander seed

1 teaspoon freshly ground canela

1/4 teaspoon freshly ground cloves or allspice

1 teaspoon coarse salt, or to taste

2 1/4 pounds (about 36-sized, 16 to 20 per pound) extra large shrimp, peeled, with the tails left on, and deveined

To make the marinade for this savory dish, you will need a seasoning paste made from annatto seeds and ground spices called Achiote Condimentado. This orange-red paste is very popular in the Yucatan. You can find this unique ingredient in Hispanic markets as well as at the Santa Fe School of Cooking. If you wish to make your own paste, refer to page 121 for a recipe. This dish goes nicely with Mexican Rice (page 132), Pickled Red Onions for a garnish (page 115), and Chipotle Sauce (page 112). This marinade is good with shellfish (especially shrimp and scallops) and grilled fish.

1. Heat the oil in a skillet over medium-high heat and sauté the cloves of garlic for 4 minutes, or until deep golden brown and softened. Cool and transfer the garlic and oil to a food processor.
2. Add the achiote, citrus juices, vinegar, water, ground spices, and salt. Process until smooth. Pour the mixture into a large bowl, add the shrimp, and toss to coat with the marinade. Cover the bowl with plastic wrap and refrigerate overnight.
3. Soak 12 8-inch wooden skewers in water for 20 minutes. Preheat a grill or broiler with the rack 4 inches from the heat. Thread 3 of the shrimp through the middle and the tail on each skewer. They should form three "C" shapes in a row.
4. Grill or broil the shrimp about 2 minutes on each side, until cooked through. Serve 2 skewers per person.

Ancho Chicken Breasts

YIELD: 4 SERVINGS

2 teaspoons
minced shallot

1 teaspoon minced garlic

2 tablespoons ground
ancho chile

Juice of 1 lime

1 teaspoon freshly
ground black pepper

2 teaspoons salt

1/2 cup olive oil

4 skinless, boneless
chicken breasts

Chef Jeff Pufal created this chicken dish for one of our culinary tour classes and it was a smashing hit with the guests. It is served at the Cooking School with a Cascabel Cumberland Sauce (see page 108 for recipe).

1. Combine all ingredients, except chicken, in a small bowl. Place the chicken breasts in a glass casserole dish and cover with the marinade. Let the chicken stand for 2 to 3 hours, covered, in the refrigerator.
2. Cook the breasts over a hot grill for 2 minutes on each side until done.

Flautas with Chorizo, Potatoes, and Chipotle Chiles

YIELD: 6 SERVINGS

3/4 pound uncooked chorizo sausage, casings removed (see page 124 for recipe)

1 pound Yellow Finn, Yukon Gold, or White Rose potatoes, peeled

3 tablespoons canola oil, plus additional oil for frying

1/3 cup slivered white onion

1 to 2 teaspoons coarse salt, to taste

3 Chipotle Chiles in Adobo Sauce, chopped, plus 2 to 3 teaspoons of the juice

12 Fresh Corn Tortillas (see page 100 for recipe)

Sour cream and Pickled Red Onions for garnish (see page 115 for recipe)

These "flutes" are corn tortillas filled, rolled, secured with toothpicks, fried until crisp and golden, and then drained on paper towels. Also known as taquitos, they are served with shredded lettuce and fresh salsa and should be eaten immediately or they become tough.

1. In a skillet over medium heat, crumble the chorizo and cook, stirring occasionally, for 8 to 10 minutes, until thoroughly cooked. Drain well on paper towels.
2. Slice the potatoes 1/4 inch thick. Cut each slice into 1/4-inch sticks.
3. Heat 3 tablespoons oil in a large skillet over medium-high heat and cook the potatoes, stirring frequently, for 5 minutes, until they begin to brown. Add the onion and salt and cook for 3 to 5 minutes more, until the potatoes are softened. Remove the skillet from the heat and stir in the chiles, juice, and chorizo.
4. Preheat the oven to 350 degrees. Wrap the tortillas in aluminum foil and warm them for 15 minutes.
5. Place 1/4 cup of the filling down the center of a tortilla and roll up tightly. Secure with a toothpick and reserve. Repeat with remaining tortillas and filling.
6. Heat 1/2 inch of the canola oil over medium-high heat to a temperature of 370 degrees. Preheat the oven to 200 degrees.
7. Fry the flautas, two at a time, for 2 to 3 minutes per side, until crisp and golden. Transfer the flautas to paper towels to drain and keep them warm in the oven until ready to serve. Repeat with remaining flautas.
8. Remove toothpicks and serve the flautas, 2 per person, garnished with sour cream and Pickled Red Onions.

Enchiladas Suizas with Salsa Verde

YIELD: 6 SERVINGS

Unlike the typical Enchiladas Suizas in the States, made with spinach or hearty greens and Swiss cheese topped with sour cream, the Mexican variety is served with a distinctive green sauce made from tomatillos.

1. Heat the chicken broth in a small saucepan and add the chicken. Bring to a boil, reduce the heat, and simmer, uncovered, for 10 minutes. Remove the pan from the heat and let the chicken cool in the broth. Shred the chicken and reserve.

2. Heat 3 tablespoons canola oil in a skillet over medium-high heat and sauté the onion 3 minutes, until softened. Add the garlic and sauté 2 minutes

3 cups chicken broth
or water

1 pound skinless,
boneless chicken breasts

3 tablespoons canola oil,
plus additional oil for
frying

1/2 cup finely chopped
white onion

2 teaspoons
minced garlic

3 to 4 minced serrano
chiles (optional)

1/4 cup coarsely
chopped cilantro

Salsa Verde

1/2 cup creme fraîche

Salt to taste

18 corn tortillas

1 cup crumbled queso
anejo or a lightly salted
feta cheese

more. Add the chiles, cilantro, and chicken, and stir
to combine well. Remove from the heat.

3. Heat the Salsa Verde in a small saucepan over
medium heat for 5 minutes. Stir in the creme fraîche
and salt to taste. Reduce the heat to low.

4. Preheat the oven to 350 degrees. Heat about 1/2-
inch of the canola oil in a skillet over medium-high
heat to 370 degrees. Fry each tortilla, submerged in
the oil, for 3 to 4 seconds, until softened but not
crispy. Transfer the tortillas to paper towels to drain.

5. Dip a fried tortilla in the sauce and transfer to a
plate. Place about 2 tablespoons of the filling down
the center of the tortilla. Roll tightly. Transfer the
rolled enchilada, seam-side down, to a 13 x 9 x 2-
inch baking dish spread with 1 cup of the green
sauce. Repeat this process with the remaining tortillas, and arrange the enchiladas in one layer in the
dish.

6. Pour the remaining sauce over the enchiladas and
cover with foil. Bake 20 minutes, or until heated
through.

7. Remove the dish from the oven and remove the
foil. Preheat the broiler and sprinkle the enchiladas
with cheese. Broil 4 inches from the heat for 2 to 3
minutes, until lightly browned. Serve immediately.

SALSA VERDE:

MAKES 4 CUPS

1 3/4 pounds tomatillos,
husked and rinsed

1 1/2 cups chopped
white onions

4 large garlic cloves,
peeled

3 to 4 jalapeño chiles,
optional or to taste

3 tablespoons canola oil

1/3 cup coarsely
chopped fresh cilantro

Coarse salt and freshly
ground pepper to taste

Pinch of sugar

1. Preheat the oven to 450 degrees. In a bowl toss
the tomatillos, onion, garlic, chiles, oil, salt, and
pepper to taste. Transfer the mixture to a small baking pan and roast in the oven for 20 to 30 minutes,
until lightly browned. Remove from the oven and
cool in the pan.

2. Add the roasted tomatillo mixture to a food
processor and pulse to a coarse purée. Add the
cilantro and season to taste with salt and sugar.
Cover and chill. This sauce will keep for up to 3 days.

Fiesta Taco on Indian Fry Bread

YIELD: 6 SERVINGS

INDIAN FRY BREAD:

2 cups flour

2 teaspoons baking powder

1/2 teaspoon salt

3/4 cup hot water

Vegetable oil for frying

FIESTA TACO TOPPINGS:

3 cups cooked ground beef, seasoned with salt and ground red chile

3 cups shredded lettuce

2 cups grated cheddar or Monterey Jack cheese

2 cups diced tomatoes

1 cup Guacamole (see page 30 for recipe)

1 cup diced onion

During Indian Market in August and Fiesta in September, downtown Santa Fe turns into a fast-food lover's delight. However, the fast food is regional in nature. Foods which you do not see on many menus such as chicharrones (fried pork skins), burritos, and Indian Tacos are served in mass quantities. I always look forward to my Indian Taco on the Plaza. It signifies the start of Fiesta, a weekend filled with friends, fun, and frivolity. The following is a basic recipe for a dish that is still served in many pueblos and certainly at the Navajo Nation. This is an open-faced taco served flat with the toppings sprinkled in layers over the top.

1. Mix together the flour, baking powder, and salt. Add the hot water and mix until all the liquid is absorbed.
2. Work the dough by hand for 10 minutes until it is soft and elastic. Cover with plastic wrap and let rest for 15 minutes.
3. Form the dough into 2-inch balls and roll to a thickness of 1/4 inch.
4. Heat 2 inches of vegetable oil in a saucepan and heat to 370 degrees. Deep fry the dough for 1 minute on each side, or until puffed and lightly golden. It is important for the oil to be hot enough to seal the dough as soon as it is dropped into it to keep the dough from absorbing oil. Place the fried bread on paper towels to drain the oil. Repeat with the remaining dough. Keep warm until ready to serve.

ASSEMBLY:

1. Place 1/4 cup of the seasoned ground beef on top of each piece of bread. Sprinkle a layer of lettuce over the beef, and then a layer of cheese and tomato. Garnish with a spoonful of guacamole and sprinkle with diced onion. Serve immediately.

Lime Marinated Grilled Salmon

YIELD: 6 TO 8 SERVINGS

LIME MARINADE:

1/3 cup freshly squeezed lime juice

2 cups coarsely chopped onion

1 1/2 teaspoons coarsely chopped garlic

2 large jalapeños, minced

1 bunch cilantro, coarsely chopped

1 tablespoon honey

1 teaspoon salt

2 pounds salmon fillets, cut in 4- to 5-ounce portions

This was the entree for our first Contemporary Southwest Cooking class and is still a favorite. However, the recipe has changed over the years. The oil in the marinade has been eliminated with no loss of flavor. It is typically served at the School with a Ginger-Lime Butter and a Corn, Tomato, and Black Bean Salsa.

1. Combine marinade ingredients in the workbowl of a food processor and pulse for 30 seconds. Taste and adjust seasoning.
2. Pour half the marinade over the bottom of a glass or stainless steel baking dish. Place the fillets on the marinade and pour the remaining marinade to cover the fillets. Marinate for at least 1 hour at room temperature or refrigerate overnight.
3. Wipe the marinade from the salmon, sprinkle the fish with salt and pepper to taste, and grill the salmon to desired doneness.

Orange-Marinated Chicken

YIELD: 6 SERVINGS

MARINADE:

3 large seedless oranges, unpeeled, cut into eighths

1 medium onion, cut into eighths

1/2 of a 7-ounce can chipotle peppers in adobo sauce

3 garlic cloves

1/3 cup chopped cilantro

4 sprigs fresh rosemary, leaves reserved, or 2 teaspoons dried

4 sprigs fresh thyme, leaves reserved, or 1 teaspoon dried

4 sprigs fresh marjoram or oregano, leaves reserved, or 2 teaspoons dried

1 teaspoon kosher salt

6 skinless, boneless chicken breasts (4 ounces each), trimmed of all fat and pounded to a thickness of 1/2 inch

Salt to taste

Vegetable cooking spray

This recipe was written by Kathi Long, one of the teachers here at the Santa Fe School of Cooking. Mexican Light is one of the most popular classes at the School, as so many people are trying to cook in a healthy way. After trying some of the recipes, you will be convinced that you do not have to sacrifice flavor to reduce fat and calories.*

1. In a food processor, combine the oranges, onion, chipotle peppers, garlic, cilantro, the reserved herb leaves, and the salt. Pulse until all the ingredients are thoroughly combined and the result is a rather coarse purée.
2. Pour half the marinade into the bottom of a non-reactive dish large enough to hold the chicken breasts in one layer. Arrange the chicken in the pan and pour the remaining marinade over the chicken. Cover the dish with plastic wrap and marinate the chicken in the refrigerator 12 to 24 hours.
3. Clean the marinade from the chicken by hand and season with salt, if needed.
4. Coat a cast-iron grill pan with vegetable cooking spray. Heat over high heat until a drop of water sizzles upon contact, about 3 minutes. Reduce the heat to medium-high, add the chicken breasts, and cook until nicely browned on one side, 3 to 5 minutes. If you like, rotate the chicken 45 degrees about halfway through cooking to create crisscross grill marks. Turn the chicken over and cook until the chicken is browned on the bottom and done throughout but still juicy, 4 to 5 minutes. Serve.

MAKING "LIGHT" OF SOUTHWESTERN COOKING

Normally the amount of fat can be decreased in a recipe. One way to do this is to use vegetable cooking spray in a non-stick skillet to sauté ingredients instead of using oil or butter. Where heavy cream or whipping cream is called for in a recipe, try to substitute a lower-fat milk product (with the exception of whipped cream as a dessert topping).

If cheese is called for, substitute a lesser quantity of the real thing. There are instances where a "dry" or aged form of the specified cheese can be substituted, and because of the intensity of the flavor you can use less (i.e., parmesan, aged goat cheese, dry jack cheese, aged asiago, aged provolone). Cheeses labeled "low fat" have better melting properties than non-fat varieties. The fact is, when you remove the fat from cheese, you no longer have "cheese," so your best bet is to use less of the real thing.

Kathi Long, author of *Mexican Light Cooking*

*Though modified to reduce the fat even further, a variation of this recipe appears in *Mexican Light Cooking*, published by Perigee Books, a division of Putnam Publishing Company.

YIELD:
10 TO 12 SERVINGS

1/2 pound lard or vegetable shortening

6 chiles anchos, stemmed and seeded

6 chiles mulatos, stemmed and seeded

8 chiles pasillas, stemmed and seeded

1 ripe plantain, peeled and cut in half lengthwise

1/2 cup raisins

1/2 cup dried apricots

6 ripe plum tomatoes

1 large onion, thickly sliced

4 large garlic cloves, peeled

1/2 cup toasted sesame seeds

1/3 cup dry roasted peanuts

1/3 cup toasted almonds

1/3 cup toasted pumpkin seeds

3 ounces tortilla chips (about 2 cups)

1/3 cup cider vinegar

4 3-ounce tablets Mexican chocolate or 12 ounces bittersweet chocolate, coarsely chopped (see Mexican Chocolate on page 171)

1/4 teaspoon ground cloves or allspice

2 teaspoons freshly ground coriander seed

2 teaspoons freshly ground anise seed

2 teaspoons freshly ground canela

10 cups chicken broth, heated

1 8- to 10-pound turkey, or one 6-pound turkey breast

Salt to taste

Roast Turkey with Mole Poblano

Mole poblano originated in the state of Puebla in Mexico, and this recipe is part of our Cuisines of Mexico class designed by Kathi Long. Mole is a rich, complex sauce thickened, more often than not, with ground seeds or nuts. Moles are of many varieties. If you have not tried mole before, you are in for a real treat.

1. Heat the lard in a saucepan over medium-high heat. Add the chiles in batches and fry them for about 40 seconds, or until puffed. Do not fry them for too long or they will burn and taste bitter. Transfer them to a large bowl and soak, weighted down, in very hot water to cover for 30 minutes, or until softened.
2. In the same pan, fry the plantain, the raisins, and the apricots in batches, removing them from the oil with a slotted spoon. Set aside. Strain the lard into a bowl and reserve.
3. Place the soaked chiles in batches in a blender and purée with 1 to 2 cups of the soaking water until smooth. The sauce should have the consistency of heavy cream. Strain to remove solids, if desired.
4. Preheat the broiler and broil the tomatoes, onion, and garlic on a baking sheet 3 inches from the heat for 2 to 3 minutes, or until browned. Turn the vegetables over and broil another 2 to 3 minutes, until browned. Let the vegetables cool.

THE ORIGIN OF MOLE POBLANO

There are numerous versions of the incident responsible for the invention of mole poblano. The most often told tale is of Sister Andrea de la Ascencia at Puebla's Santa Rosa Convent, renowned for its fine cuisine, who was asked by the bishop to create a dish unlike any they had ever tasted for a visit by the Spanish Viceroy. Sister de la Ascencia selected fresh spices, several varieties of dried Mexican chiles, fried sesame seeds, almonds, peanuts, and the definitive touch, bitter Puebla chocolate. And with that, mole poblano was born.

5. In a blender, combine the vegetables, plantain, dried fruits, seeds, nuts, tortilla chips, vinegar, chocolate, and spices in batches and purée until smooth, adding soaking liquid to adjust the consistency of the purée.

6. Heat the reserved lard in a 6-quart pot over medium-high heat. Add the chile purée and the vegetable purée, whisking to combine well, taking care as the mixture can spatter. Whisk in 8 cups of broth, adding more broth if needed. Reduce the heat to low and simmer, uncovered, stirring frequently, for 1 hour or until the sauce is thick but pourable.

7. Remove the pot from the heat and let stand at room temperature for about 1 1/2 hours. Cover and refrigerate overnight.

8. Preheat the oven to 350 degrees. Bake the turkey for about 2 hours, or until just cooked through. Let the turkey cool to room temperature, remove the skin, and remove the meat from the bones in whole pieces. Cut into 1/4-inch-thick slices and cover with plastic wrap.

9. Heat 8 cups of the sauce in a saucepan over medium heat. If the sauce is too thick, thin it with warm stock. Add turkey and heat through. Serve on a platter and sprinkle with toasted sesame seeds for garnish.

TURKEYS IN THE SOUTHWEST

Turkeys are wild birds that can be seen even today in the mountains of northern New Mexico. They date back to the Anasazi Indians. Wild turkeys, smaller than domesticated birds, are hunted in the present day in the spring and fall. The two varieties found in New Mexico are the Merriam and the Rio Grande. If you are lucky enough to have access to a wild bird, try it with mole. The slightly gamey flavor of the meat works extremely well with the richness of the mole poblano.

Stuffed Poblano Chile with Red Chile Sauce

YIELD: 6 TO 8 SERVINGS

6 to 8 large, fresh poblano chiles, roasted, peeled, and seeded

Chef Todd Sanson created this recipe for our Southwest Vegetarian class. You do not have to be vegetarian to enjoy this lively entree with contrasts in taste, color, and texture.

STUFFING:

1 tablespoon olive oil

1/2 cup finely chopped onion

1 cup corn kernels, fresh or frozen

1/2 cup toasted piñon nuts

1/2 cup golden raisins, soaked in hot water for 20 minutes

1 cup shredded Monterey Jack cheese, plus 1/2 cup for topping

1 cup soft goat cheese or goat curd

1 cup diced tofu

1/3 cup coarsely chopped fresh cilantro

Salt to taste

1. Preheat the oven to 350 degrees.
2. Mix all stuffing ingredients together in a bowl. Season to taste.
3. Stuff each poblano chile with some of the cheese mixture and place on a lightly oiled baking sheet.
4. Sprinkle the chiles with the additional cheese and bake in the oven until heated through, about 15 to 20 minutes.

RED CHILE SAUCE:

1/4 cup olive or vegetable oil

1/2 cup finely diced onion

1 teaspoon minced garlic

2 teaspoons freshly ground canela

2 teaspoons freshly ground coriander seed

1 cup pure ground Chimayo red chile

2 2-ounce tablets Mexican chocolate

3 1/2 to 4 cups water

1 1/2 tablespoons vinegar

1 1/2 teaspoons salt, or to taste

1. Heat the olive oil in a saucepan over medium-high heat. Sauté the onions until softened, about 2 minutes. Add the garlic and sauté about 2 minutes.
2. Add the remaining ingredients and simmer over low heat for 15 minutes, stirring occasionally, until the mixture has thickened.
3. When the chiles are heated through, place 1 to 2 ounces of the sauce on each plate and place a stuffed poblano on top of the sauce.

FRESH GOAT CHEESE

A regular at Santa Fe's Farmer's Market is Patrice Harrison-Inglis of Sweetwoods Dairy. Patrice, her husband Harrison, and their two sons started the dairy in 1992 with 26 milkers and one billy on five acres in the rural area of Peña Blanca. From their Grade A approved dairy, they process and package goat cheese of exceptional quality. The goats are milked twice daily, and the milk is made into fresh cheese each morning. According to Patrice, "gently processing milk preserves its delicate qualities. Fresh cheese really means unripened or unaged." The fresh cheese is then wrapped to allow it to breathe, preserving the activity of the cultures in it and allowing the possibility of aging. The cheese should be eaten within 10 days to two weeks for a fresh, mild-flavored goat cheese. In the Vegetarian Stuffed Poblano recipe, we use an unflavored goat cheese. However, Patrice flavors some of the cheese with a variety of spices and herbs, including green chile, basil, and ground pepper. The end results make wonderful and easy appetizers. These cheeses are great with sandwiches, omelettes, and blended soups. The cheeses with herbs and peppercorn crusts work well with fresh green salads or spread on fish or eggplant for grilling. We include these marvelous cheeses in the wine-tastings, which are part of the School's culinary tours.

Blue corn meal in molcajete and an antique wood tortilla press

SOUTHWESTERN

Breads and Muffins

The most common bread served in Santa Fe is the tortilla, which is served either as an accompaniment to a meal or in such dishes as tacos, chalupas, enchiladas, and burritos. Essential to the mastery of the cuisine of Santa Fe is the ability to make both flour and corn tortillas. Students at the School and readers of this book will learn to create both corn and flour tortillas. Also included in this chapter are recipes for the much revered sopaipilla and for hearty blue corn muffins.

Blue Corn Muffins with Chile and Cheese

YIELD: 1 DOZEN LARGE MUFFINS OR 18 SMALL MUFFINS

1/2 cup softened butter

1/2 cup sugar

5 large eggs

1/2 cup buttermilk (milk may be substituted)

1 cup all-purpose flour

1 cup blue cornmeal

2 teaspoons baking powder

1 teaspoon salt

1 cup fresh or frozen corn kernels

1 cup grated Monterey Jack cheese

1 cup grated cheddar cheese

3/4 cup roasted, peeled, diced green chile

This recipe is one of the most popular recipes of the Cooking School. It is part of our Traditional New Mexican III class and is simple enough that it has also been used for kids' cooking classes. You can make these muffins ahead of time as they reheat very well.

1. Preheat oven to 375 degrees. Grease muffin tins well or insert paper liners.
2. In the bowl of an electric mixer, cream together the butter and sugar until smooth. In a separate bowl, whisk together the eggs and buttermilk.
3. In another bowl, mix together the dry ingredients. Add the dry ingredients to the butter and sugar. In a separate bowl, whisk together the eggs and buttermilk. Slowly mix wet ingredients into the dry ingredients.
4. Stir in the corn, cheese, and chiles and mix well. Spoon the batter into muffin tins. Bake about 25 minutes, until just firm. Serve warm with butter.

VARIATION:

For a more savory muffin, reduce the sugar to 1/2 cup and add 1/2 cup diced onion and 1 tablespoon minced garlic sautéed in 2 tablespoons olive or vegetable oil and 1 tablespoon Chimayo ground red chile to the batter when the corn and cheese are added. Omit the green chile. The results are superb.

USING FRESH CORN

Fresh corn kernels add wholesome flavor and textural interest to these muffins. When slicing the kernels off the cob, take care not to cut too deeply or you will detach too much of the unchewable cellulose.

Sopaipillas

1 cup flour

1/2 teaspoon salt

3/4 teaspoon baking powder

1 tablespoon sugar

2 teaspoons vegetable shortening

1/2 cup water or milk

Canola oil for frying

These puffy, golden "sofa pillows" of deep-fried leavened dough are a New Mexican specialty. They are enjoyed as an accompaniment to savory foods, often stuffed with meat or beans, or as a dessert with honey.

1. Combine the flours, salt, baking powder, and sugar in a bowl. Cut in the shortening until a coarse meal is formed.
2. Stir in the water with a fork until the mixture comes together into a moist dough. Form into a ball, knead several times, cover, and let stand for 30 minutes.
3. Heat the oil in a deep pot to 375 degrees.
4. Roll out half of the dough and cut into 3- to 4-inch squares or triangles. Drop the pieces of dough, one by one, into the hot oil and fry until golden, about 30 to 40 seconds, rolling them over to brown on both sides. Roll, cut, and fry remaining dough in the same manner. Drain on paper towels and serve warm with honey or honey butter.

ENSURING LIGHT AND FLUFFY SOPAIPILLAS

You want these delicacies to be as airy as pillows, so be sure to handle the dough lightly so as to keep it tender, allow it to rest, and maintain the 375-degree oil temperature by cooking only 3 or 4 sopaipillas at a time. If your sopaipillas are not puffing immediately after dropping them into the hot oil, try holding them under the oil with a slotted spoon for a few seconds until they puff, and then continue rolling and browning on both sides to cook. The sopaipillas will collapse quickly as they cool, so plan to serve immediately after cooking.

USING PANOCHA FLOUR

For a richer flavor and more interesting texture, substitute 1/4 cup panocha flour for 1/4 cup white flour. Panocha is a slightly sweet sprouted wheat flour used traditionally in New Mexico during Lent to make a dessert, also called panocha. My favorite use of this flour is to add it to sopaipilla dough. It adds a wonderful texture and a whole-wheat flavor to the sopaipillas.

Few restaurants have panocha on the menu as a dessert. However, in the mountain village of Truchas is the Truchas Mountain Cafe, which always has the dessert panocha on the menu. I highly recommend stopping at this authentic northern New Mexico restaurant. I frequently take culinary tours there, where I coax the owner and cook, Josephine Romero, to demonstrate the making of her incredible sopaipillas. For years I have quizzed her for her recipe. Finally she confessed that, with each batch of sopaipilla dough, she says a blessing. This is her secret ingredient, although I suspect she is also adding panocha flour.

MAKE YOUR OWN PANOCHA FLOUR

Orlando Casados farms on 47 acres of irrigated land in El Guique about 7 miles north of Española. In addition to raising the crops, Orlando and his sister Deloris process products such as posole, chicos, corn meal, and chiles in the old, traditional ways. Here Orlando shares his recipe for panocha flour:

Soak whole wheat overnight. Wash and drain it and then put it in a cloth bag. Keep the grain moist by covering the sack with plastic. Store at room temperature until the grain sprouts (2 to 3 days). Spread the sprouted wheat out in a well-ventilated or sunny place to dry, occasionally turning the grain to prevent molding. When the wheat is dry, grind to a fine flour.

Fresh Corn Tortillas

YIELD: ABOUT 16 4-INCH TORTILLAS

2 cups Masa Harina
(See Masa)

1/2 teaspoon salt

1 1/3 cups (approximately)
warm water

Making corn tortillas from scratch is much less common in Santa Fe than making flour tortillas. There is nothing that makes a recipe as authentic—and delicious—as using fresh corn tortillas. Corn tortillas are easy to make and are even good plain. In fact, I often start my day off at the Cooking School by pouring myself a cup of freshly brewed coffee and eating one of the corn tortillas that the prep cook is making for the day's class.

1. Place the dry ingredients in a medium bowl and slowly add the water, stirring with a fork until the dough comes together into a ball. Knead the dough several times and roll into a log shape about 2 inches in diameter and 8 inches long. Wrap the log in plastic wrap and let it stand for about 30 minutes.
2. Preheat a cast iron comal, skillet, or griddle over medium-high heat. Cut the log into 1/2-inch rounds, keeping the rounds covered so that the dough doesn't dry out. Place one of the rounds between 2 sheets of plastic in a tortilla press and flatten to about 1/16-inch thick. Peel off the plastic and place the tortilla in the preheated pan. Cook about 1 minute, until light brown speckles appear. Flip the tortilla and cook half a minute, pressing down on the tortilla with a small spatula. Repeat with the remaining rounds. As the tortillas are cooked, stack them in a kitchen towel to keep warm. Serve immediately.

USING A FOOD PROCESSOR

This recipe may also be made in a food processor. Place the dry ingredients in the workbowl fitted with the steel blade. While the machine is running, slowly pour the warm water through the feed tube and process until the dough forms a ball. Proceed as directed above.

USING A TORTILLA PRESS

In today's New Mexican household, most corn tortillas are made with cast iron or aluminum tortilla presses. Some of the local antique stores offer well-worn, mesquite-wood presses that are charming and quite usable. The heavier cast-iron models are sturdiest and provide the best results. A tortilla press is a very useful piece of equipment for the time-conscious cook who enjoys making fresh tortillas. Cast-iron presses can often be found in Hispanic markets, or they can be ordered through the Cooking School.

MASA

Masa is the name given to dough made from ground posole (see page 139). If you are lucky enough to live in an area where there is a tortilla factory, you can probably find fresh masa. Fresh masa is extremely perishable and should be used within a day. It can also be frozen, well-wrapped, for up to a month.

In some parts of the country you can find a dried version of masa. Stone ground with no additives, masa harina is available through the School of Cooking under the Santa Fe School of Cooking label.

Flour Tortillas of the Rancho

YIELD:
12 TO 14 TORTILLAS

4 cups all-purpose flour

1/2 teaspoon baking powder

4 tablespoons canola oil

1 1/2 teaspoons salt

1 1/2 cups warm water

Flour tortillas from California and Arizona are very different from the thick ones common in New Mexico. Jacqueline Higuera McMahan shared her secrets for making Rancho-style tortillas on one of her visits to Santa Fe when she was a guest chef at the Santa Fe School of Cooking.*

1. Sift flour and baking powder together. Remove 1/2 cup of the flour mixture and use a fork to blend the canola oil into this flour. When well-blended, place in a plastic bag and freeze for an hour.

2. Use a fork to blend the cold flour-oil mixture into the dry flour mixture until it resembles pastry crumbs. Mix the salt into the warm water and drizzle the water into the flour mixture until you can make a soft ball of dough. Knead the dough for 1 minute in the bowl. Cover with plastic wrap and let stand for 30 minutes to 2 hours at room temperature.

3. Oil a jelly roll pan and then form the dough into 14 balls. Flatten the balls into 3-inch discs and allow them to rest for 30 minutes, covered in plastic wrap. These two resting periods not only help the dough mellow but also to relax so it is much easier to work with.

4. Preheat a griddle or comal. Dust a floured board and place a flattened tortilla ball in the center. Roll

the dough into a circle, rolling from the center out. Make a quarter turn of the tortilla after each 2 strokes so the tortilla will remain round. The perfect tool for rolling is a sawed-off, clean broom handle or a 7-inch piece of wooden dowel.

5. After you have rolled the tortilla to an 8-inch circle, handstretch it to a 10-inch circle. Hang the tortilla from the fingertips of one hand (if you are right-handed, drape the tortilla from your left hand, and vice-versa) and draw the fingers of the opposing hand underneath the tortilla. The fingers should pull and stretch in a gentle fashion. Do this a couple of times in each direction. You will have a delicately thin tortilla than cannot be achieved by rolling it on a board.

6. Place the tortilla on a heated comal or griddle over medium heat. Keep turning the tortilla every 10 seconds. It will get light brown freckles and puff in spots. Do not push on the tortilla when it is puffing as this is just the formation of delicate layers. You will have to turn it 4 or 5 times on the comal. When the tortilla stops puffing, it is done. A homemade flour tortilla cooks in less than a minute. If you overcook tortillas they become very dry. Place the cooked tortillas inside a tea towel. Do not place in plastic or they will sweat.

*This recipe is from her cookbook *California Rancho Cooking* (The Olive Press, 1988).

Fresh Flour Tortillas

**YIELD: 8 TO 10
5-INCH TORTILLAS**

2 cups flour

1 teaspoon salt

3 teaspoons baking powder

2 tablespoons vegetable shortening

3/4 to 1 cup hot water

Flour tortillas are very common in northern New Mexico, and they are quite thick. In many homes, fresh flour tortillas are made on a daily basis and used in place of bread. Flour tortillas are somewhat more difficult to make than corn tortillas, with the handling of the dough being the tricky part.

1. Combine the dry ingredients in a bowl and mix well. Cut in the shortening until a coarse meal is formed. Add enough water to make a very soft, but not sticky, dough. Knead about 15 times into a smooth ball. Divide the dough equally into 8 to 10 balls. Cover the dough balls and let stand for about 20 minutes.

2. To flatten, take one ball of dough and, beginning in the middle of the ball, roll away from you, turning the dough a quarter turn after each roll. You will want a circle about 5 inches in diameter. Proceed with the remaining dough balls.

3. Preheat a cast iron comal, skillet, or griddle to medium-high. Place a flattened tortilla on the heated surface and cook about 15 seconds, pressing down on the round with a small spatula. As the tortilla takes on a lightly browned, speckled appearance, flip it to the other side and continue to cook another 20 seconds. Place the finished tortillas in a kitchen towel to keep warm. Serve immediately.

USING A COMAL

The comal, which means griddle in Spanish, was originally made of clay but is now made of cast iron or steel. The cast iron comals are most commonly available in Hispanic markets. A well-seasoned comal is the ideal piece of equipment to use for cooking flour and corn tortillas because it can be heated evenly to a very high temperature.

Pickled Red Onions, Salsa Fresca, and Guacamole

Spicy SAUCES, Sizzling SALSAS, and Snappy RELISHES

There is probably no section of this book more important than the chapter on sauces, salsas, and relishes. Good sauces provide the basis for traditional foods such as enchiladas while piquant salsas perfectly compliment more contemporary dishes. A simple grilled chicken breast can be made into a mouth-watering delight with the fiery flavors of salsas and relishes. Control the heat level of these sauces, salsas, and relishes by choosing the appropriate chile or by using less of the chile.

Cabbage and Apple Garnish

YIELD: 4 SERVINGS

1 cup shredded
red cabbage

1/4 Granny Smith apple,
diced

1/4 Red Delicious apple,
diced

1 tablespoon
sherry vinegar

1 tablespoon sugar

Salt to taste

Cabbage and apples make a festive fall garnish
and go particularly well with pork. This colorful
version is part of our Contemporary Southwest
III class.

1. In a small, non-reactive bowl, combine all ingredients and mix thoroughly. Refrigerate until ready
to use.

USING A MANDOLINE

A mandoline is a kitchen
tool for slicing, finely
shredding, and julienning
that can greatly reduce
the prep time for gar-
nishes such as this.
Commercial varieties can
run well over $100; how-
ever, inexpensive plastic
ones work quite well for
the home cook.

Cascabel Cumberland Sauce

YIELD: 4 CUPS

2 cups raspberry preserves

1 cup red wine

1/2 cup fresh orange juice

1/3 cup fresh lemon juice

1 tablespoon minced garlic

2 teaspoons Mexican
oregano

4 dried cascabel chiles,
stemmed and seeded

This makes a wonderful sauce for chicken and
an excellent glaze for ham.

1. Mix all ingredients in a saucepan over high heat
and bring to a boil. Reduce the heat and continue to
simmer for 2 minutes. Remove from the heat and
cool. The sauce will thicken slightly. Serve the sauce
at room temperature.

Ginger-Lime Butter

YIELD:
APPROXIMATELY 1 CUP

1/4 pound butter,
softened

1 tablespoon
freshly grated ginger

1/3 cup coarsely
chopped fresh cilantro

1 1/2 teaspoons freshly
squeezed lime juice

1/2 teaspoon salt

Flavored butters keep well in the freezer and provide a quick and easy way to liven up a variety of dishes from fish and fowl to vegetables. We use this intensely flavored butter on the lime-marinated grilled salmon in our Contemporary I class.

1. Combine all the ingredients in the workbowl of a food processor and pulse until smooth. If not using within 45 minutes, refrigerate. Serve 1 teaspoon of the flavored butter on top of each portion of the salmon hot off the grill.

Green Chile Chutney

YIELD: ABOUT 2 CUPS

4 fresh tomatillos,
peeled, rinsed, and
quartered

1 cup coarsely
chopped onion

1/4 cup roasted, peeled,
seeded, and chopped
New Mexican green chile

1 cup sugar

1 cup cider vinegar

2 teaspoons salt

1/4 teaspoon freshly
ground cumin seed

1/4 teaspoon freshly
ground coriander seed

1 teaspoon pure ground
Chimayo red chile, mild
or medium

This makes a great condiment for blue corn pancakes, and it is also good with poultry and as an appetizer with cheese or cream cheese.

1. Place the tomatillos and the onion in the workbowl of a food processor and pulse until uniformly chopped. Place this mixture and the remaining ingredients in a heavy saucepan over high heat. Bring to a boil, reduce the heat, and simmer gently for 50 to 60 minutes, stirring frequently, until the mixture resembles a thick relish.

2. Cool slightly and serve.

TOMATILLOS

The tart, refreshing flavor of this fruit is the foundation of many Mexican green sauces. Occasionally used raw in a salsa, tomatillos are usually simmered or dry-roasted. Although it resembles a small green tomato in a papery husk, the tomatillo is a close relative of the cape gooseberry, which grows wild in the United States. Fresh tomatillos are often available year-round in supermarkets and specialty produce markets, although canned tomatillos make an acceptable substitute. Select small, firm, bright green tomatillos that completely fill their husks. Loosely wrapped, they keep well in the refrigerator for several weeks. Before using, remove the papery husks and rinse to remove the sticky substance on their surfaces.

Green Chile Chasseur Sauce

**YIELD:
APPROXIMATELY 4 CUPS**

1 tablespoon butter

2 tablespoons olive oil

3/4 cup chopped onion

1 teaspoon minced garlic

12 ounces mushrooms, diced

2 tablespoons flour

1 1/4 cups diced ripe tomatoes

1/2 cup roasted, peeled, chopped green chile

2 cups chicken stock

1 teaspoon
dried tarragon

1 to 1 1/2 teaspoons salt

This classic French game sauce, spiced with green chiles, makes a nice accompaniment to fowl of any type. We typically serve this over our Oven Baked Cornish Game Hen (page 81), and it also complements quail, dove, or chicken.

1. In a medium skillet over medium heat, melt the butter and add the oil. Add the onion and sauté for 3 minutes, stirring frequently. Add the garlic and sauté 1 minute.

2. Add the mushrooms and cook 3 minutes. Add the flour and stir to combine well. Add the tomatoes, chile, stock, and tarragon and stir. Reduce the heat to low and simmer for about 1 hour.

3. Add salt to taste.

Green Chile Sauce

YIELD: 2 1/2 CUPS

1/4 cup vegetable oil

1 cup chopped onion

2 to 3 teaspoons minced garlic, to taste

1 tablespoon flour

2/3 cup mild roasted, peeled, chopped New Mexican green chile

2/3 cup hot roasted, peeled, chopped New Mexican green chile

2 teaspoons freshly ground coriander seed

1 1/2 cups chicken stock

Salt to taste

Use this basic sauce for Chicken or Cheese Enchiladas, or as an accompaniment to meats or fish.

1. Heat the oil in a medium saucepan and sauté the onion until softened, about 3 to 4 minutes. Add the garlic and sauté 2 minutes more. Stir in the flour.

2. Slowly stir in the chicken stock and add the green chile and ground coriander seed. Bring the mixture to a boil, reduce the heat, and simmer for about 15 minutes. Season with salt to taste.

SOME LIKE IT HOT: TAKING ON THE CHILE

When classes at the Cooking School are asked for words to describe chiles, invariably the word that comes up most often is "HOT." Aside from the fiery sensation associated with chiles, they offer a pleasing complexity of unique flavors, textures, and colors. Tasting the chiles before use is the most reliable method of adjusting the heat to your own personal comfort level. Removing the veins, seeds, and membranes from the roasted and peeled green chiles, as well as soaking them in salted ice water for half an hour, also serves to cool down the heat prior to cooking with them. However, should the occasion happen to arise when an antidote to the hotness of chiles is needed, there are several methods to reduce the heat in your mouth. Dairy products, including milk, sour cream, ice cream, or yogurt, work best to ease the burning sensation. Starchy foods, such as beans, bread, posole, potatoes, or rice also neutralize the heat, as does a spoonful of sugar. Alcoholic beverages, including beer and wine, actually increase the absorption of the heat-producing capsaicin, which in turn makes the food seem even hotter.

Remember that when you are dining in a New Mexican restaurant, and are wondering about the pungency of the different chile dishes, you can ask which chile is the hottest that day, red or green, because one is not necessarily hotter than the other.

Chipotle Sauce

**YIELD: APPROXIMATELY
1 1/2 CUPS**

1 7.5-ounce can Chipotle
Peppers in Adobo

1 cup olive oil

4 large garlic cloves,
peeled

1 large egg and 1 egg
yolk

1/2 teaspoon coarse salt,
or to taste

This smoky dipping sauce is good with fish and
shellfish (especially shrimp and scallops).

1. Place the contents of the can of Chipotle Peppers
in Adobo in a blender and purée. Sieve the purée to
remove the chile skins and seeds and reserve the
remaining purée.
2. Heat 3 tablespoons of the oil in a small skillet
over medium heat and sauté the whole garlic cloves
4 to 5 minutes, until they are deep golden brown and
softened.
3. In the workbowl of a food processor place 2 tablespoons of the reserved chile purée, 1 whole egg, 1
egg yolk, and the sautéed garlic cloves. Process to a
smooth purée, slowly adding the remaining oil. You
should end up with a sauce a little thicker than heavy
cream, but not as thick as a mayonnaise. Add salt to
taste and refrigerate until ready to use.

Chipotles in Adobo

2 quarts boiling water for soaking

1/4 pound chipotles, moras, moritas, or home-smoked chiles

4 ancho chiles

2 large tomatoes, broiled or charred over a flame

1 head garlic, top sliced off

2 bay leaves

2 teaspoon cumin seeds, mashed

1 teaspoon dried oregano

1 stick canela or cinnamon

3 whole cloves, crushed

1 sprig fresh thyme

1/2 cup apple cider vinegar

1 1/2 cups water

1 tablespoon olive oil

1 tablespoon brown sugar

1 1/2 teaspoons salt

At the Santa Fe School of Cooking Market we carry a variety of excellent brands of chipotle chiles in adobo. However, many cooks enjoy making their own. At last we have a recipe for making chipotles in adobo thanks to guest chef Jacqueline Higeuera McMahan.*

1. Pour the boiling water over the chipotles and ancho chiles. Soak for 30 minutes. Remove all the chile stems, but leave the seeds.
2. In a blender, purée 6 of the soaked chipotles, the ancho chiles, the tomatoes, and 1 cup of the soaking liquid. Place the purée in a 3-quart heavy pot with the rest of the ingredients.
3. Simmer for 45 minutes, until the chiles become unctuously soft. Store in a glass quart jar in the refrigerator for up to 2 months. The adobo sauce will thicken as it sits. You can use the adobo sauce without the chiles for a lighter chipotle flavoring or you can purée the entire batch of chipotles and sauce to give it a stronger flavor. Before puréeing, remove the cinnamon and bay leaves.

*This recipe appears in her most recent cookbook, *The Chipotle Chile Cookbook*, published by The Olive Press, 1994.

Onion and Chile Madeira Cream Sauce

YIELD: 2 CUPS

3 tablespoons butter

1/3 cup julienned red onion

1/3 cup julienned leeks, white part only

1/4 cup julienned white or yellow onion

3 teaspoons minced garlic

1 Poblano chile, roasted, peeled, seeded, and cut in thin strips

1 New Mexican green chile, roasted, peeled, seeded, and cut in thin strips

Salt and freshly ground white pepper to taste

1/2 cup Madeira

1 1/2 cups heavy cream

This rich cream sauce with a hint of chile goes well with pork dishes.

1. Heat the butter in a large skillet over medium-high heat. Add the leeks and onions and sauté for 3 minutes, until softened. Add the garlic, and continue to sauté for 3 minutes. Add the chiles and cook 2 minutes. Season with salt and white pepper.
2. Deglaze the pan with Madeira and flame by lighting the mixture with a match and allowing the alcohol to burn off. Add the cream and simmer the mixture for 8 to 12 minutes.

DEGLAZING

Deglazing is a technique in making sauces where liquid is added to the pan which has been used for cooking. When deglazing, bring the mixture to a simmer and scrape the bottom and sides of the pan in order to incorporate all the browned particles into the liquid mixture. Continue simmering and stirring until the sauce reaches the desired consistency.

Pickled Red Onions

YIELD: 4 CUPS

2 cups red wine vinegar

1 6-ounce can frozen orange juice concentrate, thawed

3/4 cup sugar

1 tablespoon dried Mexican oregano

4 bay leaves, broken in half

Salt to taste

1 1/4 pounds medium-sized red onions, peeled and cut into slivers

These onions make a wonderful garnish for fajitas, tacos, enchiladas, and salads, or you may like them so much you just eat them by themselves. They have a terrific citrus flavor and have no added oil, which makes them all the more appealing.

1. Combine all the ingredients except the onions in a large bowl and stir until the sugar is dissolved. Add the onions and combine well.

2. Cover the bowl and let the onions stand at room temperature, stirring occasionally, for 12 to 24 hours. Stir the mixture once again and then refrigerate, covered. These onions will keep for up to two weeks. After that, these onions retain their flavor but lose some of their vibrant color.

Red Chile Sauce with Dried Chile Pods

YIELD: ABOUT 3 CUPS

12 New Mexican red chile pods, preferably sun-dried

2 to 3 cups boiling water

1/4 cup vegetable oil

1 cup finely chopped onion

2 to 3 teaspoons minced garlic

1 teaspoon dried Mexican oregano

1/2 teaspoon freshly ground cumin seed

It is difficult for New Mexicans to agree about whether dried whole chile pods or dried ground chiles produce the ultimate red chile sauce. With respect for the seriousness of this argument, we take no side and have presented recipes for both. I believe that the quality of the chile, whether it be pods or powder, produces the quality of the chile sauce. It goes without saying, however, that the commercial product sold in markets as "chili powder" should be avoided for making a red chile sauce. Containing several other spices, but little pure ground chile powder, this product is meant as a seasoning for chili con carne. It cannot bring the sweet, earthy flavor that pure, ground, 100-percent New Mexican chiles bring to a red sauce.

1. Rinse the pods well. Remove the stems from the chiles and shake out the seeds. Place the pods in a bowl and cover with 2 to 3 cups of boiling water. Weight the chiles to submerge them (they have a tendency to float), and let them stand for 30 minutes.
2. In the meantime, heat the oil in a small skillet and sauté the onion for about 3 minutes, until softened. Add the garlic and cook 2 minutes. Remove from the heat and set aside.
3. Drain the soaked chiles, reserving the liquid. Place half of the chiles in a blender jar. Add about 1 1/2 cups of the soaking liquid and half of the sautéed onion/garlic mixture. Purée. Add more soaking liquid if the mixture seems too thick. Repeat the process with the remaining chiles, onions, garlic, and 1 1/2 cups of the soaking liquid.
4. Pour the purées into a medium saucepan and bring to a boil. Add oregano and ground cumin. Reduce the heat to low and simmer the mixture for about 20 minutes. Strain the sauce and discard the solids.

SUN-DRIED CHILE PODS

There are a few farmers in New Mexico who allow the pods to remain on the plants to dry rather than commercially dehydrating the chiles. This sun drying produces a sweeter chile. Workers are still picking chiles from the dry plant in February, prior to tilling the soil in preparation for the next season. Sun-dried chile pods are available most of the year through the Santa Fe School of Cooking Mail Order.

Red Chile Sauce with Ground Red Chile

YIELD:
APPROXIMATELY 3 CUPS

1/4 cup vegetable oil

1/2 cup finely diced onion

2 to 3 teaspoons minced garlic

1/2 cup pure ground medium red chile powder

2 tablespoons all-purpose flour (optional)

2 1/2 cups water

1 teaspoon dried Mexican oregano

1/2 teaspoon freshly ground cumin seed

Salt to taste

1. Heat the oil in a medium saucepan and sauté the onion for 3 to 4 minutes, until softened. Add the garlic and sauté 2 minutes more.

2. Stir in the chile (and flour if using) and slowly add the water, whisking to break up any lumps in the chile. The chile powder will thicken the sauce, but you may prefer to use flour also.

3. Add the oregano and the cumin and bring to a boil. Reduce the heat and simmer for about 20 minutes, or until the mixture has thickened slightly. Season with salt to taste.

EL ASADOR

This unique stovetop grill can be used on electric, gas, and wood stoves. Simply center El Asador on the element or gas burner of your stove. Preheat to high for 5 minutes. At this point, you can toast, roast, or grill just about anything you want. El Asador gives foods the flavor of outdoor grilling.

Roasted Tomato-Green Chile Salsa

YIELD: 2 CUPS

6 medium-sized ripe Roma tomatoes

2 large whole garlic cloves, unpeeled

1 medium red onion, finely chopped

1/3 cup mild roasted, chopped New Mexican green chile

3 tablespoons coarsely chopped fresh cilantro

1 tablespoon freshly squeezed lime juice, or to taste

Salt to taste

1. Core the tomatoes and cut an X on the bottom. Preheat El Asador over a high gas flame or an electric burner and place the tomatoes on the grill. As the tomatoes char on one side, turn them and char the next side. Repeat until the tomatoes are well charred on all sides. Remove the tomatoes to a bowl and let them cool.

2. Repeat the process with the unpeeled garlic until the skin is charred and the garlic inside is soft and caramelized. Peel the tomatoes and chop them coarsely, reserving the juice.

3. Peel the garlic cloves and mince them. Place the tomatoes, garlic, onion, green chile, and cilantro in a medium bowl. Season to taste with lime juice and salt and mix well. Let the mixture stand for 30 minutes and serve at room temperature.

ROASTING TOMATOES

An alternative method for roasting tomatoes is to place the tomatoes on a baking sheet lined with aluminum foil. Preheat the broiler to high. Place the baking sheet under the broiler and char the tomatoes on all sides. Cool, peel away the charred skin, and remove the core. The tomatoes will have a wonderful smoky aroma and flavor. Save the juice that accumulates because it also carries that flavor.

Salsa Fresca

YIELD: ABOUT 3 CUPS

4 to 5 Roma (Italian plum) tomatoes, diced

1 teaspoon minced garlic

1/2 cup finely chopped red or white onion

1/4 cup fresh lime juice

1 to 2 fresh jalapeños, seeded and finely chopped

3 tablespoons coarsely chopped fresh cilantro

1 tablespoon olive oil (optional)

Salt to taste

Salsas have become the most-used condiment in the United States, surpassing ketchup. The following is a traditional salsa which we have used for a long time at the School because of its popularity.

1. Put the tomatoes, garlic, onion, lime juice, jalapeños, and cilantro in a bowl and mix well. You may want to lightly mash the ingredients with the back of a large spoon or a potato masher to give the mixture more of a puréed texture or you can leave the ingredients intact for a chunkier salsa.
2. Add the olive oil, if using, and salt to taste. Let the mixture stand for 30 minutes to allow the flavors to develop. Serve with tostada chips or as a garnish with meats or fish.

Corn, Tomato, and Black Bean Salsa

YIELD: 2 1/2 CUPS

1/2 cup finely chopped onion

1 teaspoon minced garlic

2 tablespoons olive oil

3 tablespoons coarsely chopped fresh cilantro

1/4 teaspoon lightly toasted, freshly ground cumin seed

1 jalapeño chile, minced

2 tablespoons cider vinegar

1 tablespoon Red Chile Honey (see page 131)

1 teaspoon salt

3/4 cup fresh corn kernels

3 large ripe Roma tomatoes

1 cup cooked black beans

This makes an excellent side dish for both hot and cold entrees.

1. Lightly sauté the onion and garlic in the olive oil until soft. Place the chopped cilantro, cumin seed, jalapeño, vinegar, honey, and salt in a mixing bowl and combine well.

2. Add the corn, tomato, black beans and sautéed ingredients. Stir to combine thoroughly. Let the salsa stand for 30 to 45 minutes to blend the flavors.

Yucatecan Achiote Seasoning Paste

YIELD: 1/4 CUP

1 tablespoon achiote seeds

1 teaspoon black peppercorns (or a scant 1 1/2 teaspoons ground)

1 teaspoon dried oregano

4 cloves (or about 1/8 teaspoon ground)

1/2 teaspoon cumin seeds (or a generous 1/2 teaspoon ground)

1 teaspoon coriander seeds (or a generous teaspoon ground)

1 inch cinnamon stick or canela (or about 1 teaspoon ground)

1 scant teaspoon salt

5 cloves garlic, peeled

2 tablespoons vinegar

1 1/2 teaspoons flour

Rick Bayless of Frontera Grill in Chicago was a guest chef at the 1993 Wine and Chile Fiesta. I am delighted to include this recipe because I am asked frequently how to make Achiote Paste. Here is the answer.*

1. Measure the achiote seeds, peppercorns, oregano, cloves, cumin, cinnamon, and coriander seeds into a spice grinder and pulverize as completely as possible; it will take a minute or more, due to the hardness of the achiote. Transfer to a small bowl and mix in the salt.
2. Finely mince the garlic and sprinkle it with some of the spice mixture. Use the back of a spoon or a flexible spreader to work it back and forth into a smooth paste. Mix in the remaining spice powder and then mix in the vinegar and flour.
3. Transfer into a small jar, cover, and let stand several hours (or, preferably, overnight) before using. The paste can be finished in 15 minutes, but it should be made several hours ahead. Refrigerate if not using within 2 days. It will keep well for months.

*Guest chef Rick Bayless contributed this recipe from his book *Authentic Mexican*, published by William Morrow, 1987.

GRINDING ACHIOTE

Because achiote seeds are very hard, they are best pulverized in a high-speed spice grinder; unless they are reduced to a powder, the paste will be gritty. If you can't find a high-speed grinder, use a blender fitted with a mini-blend container. To do this, prepare a double batch, pulverizing the achiote and spices first and then blending in the garlic (roughly chopped) and, finally, the vinegar and flour. If you must use a mortar, which requires lots of energy, grind the seeds a teaspoon at a time, transferring them to a small bowl; grind the spices and then add the ground achiote, flour, and vinegar. Pound to a paste.

Posole with Blue Corn Muffins

Side Dishes,
SANTA FE STYLE

Frequently, side dishes are used to cut the heat of the fiery Southwestern foods they are served with. This is why a side of posole (lime treated corn) is often served with enchiladas and carne adovada. When your mouth feels as if it is going to explode from the heat, one bite of mild posole cures the burn. The recipes we have included in this section rely heavily on the staples of Southwestern cuisine—beans, corn, and squash—and we've added some new twists on the old American standby, the potato.

Black Beans with Garlic and Chipotle Chiles

1 pound black turtle beans (2 cups), picked over for stones

2 tablespoons vegetable oil or olive oil

1 cup chopped onion

2 teaspoons minced garlic

4 bay leaves

2 teaspoons Mexican oregano

2 teaspoons dried epazote

3 dried chipotle chiles

4 to 5 quarts water

4 tablespoons vinegar, to taste

1 to 2 teaspoons salt, to taste

2 tablespoons Amontillado Sherry

This recipe is part of the Southwest Vegetarian class developed by Todd Sanson. These beans make a great side dish, or they can be used as a filling for burritos.

1. Soak the beans in water to cover overnight.
2. Heat the oil in a 4-quart pot and sauté the onion for 3 minutes. Add the garlic and continue cooking for 2 minutes. Add the bay leaves, oregano, epazote, and chiles and sauté for 1 minute. Add 3 quarts of the water and bring to a boil. Reduce the heat and simmer, uncovered, for 2 to 3 hours, or until the beans are soft. Add the remaining quart of water as needed during cooking.
3. Add the vinegar and salt and continue to cook slowly for 30 minutes more. Taste and adjust seasonings.
4. Stir in the sherry before serving. Serve or reserve for later use.

Chorizo (Mexican Sausage)

1 pound lean pork, coarsely ground

1 1/2 teaspoons salt

2 tablespoons pure ground red chile, or more to taste

4 cloves garlic, minced

1 teaspoon Mexican oregano

3/4 teaspoon ground canela or cinnamon

1/2 teaspoon ground cloves

1/4 cup ground paprika

1/4 cup red wine or cider vinegar

If you cannot find a good brand of chorizo in your grocery store, you can make your own using Janet Mitchell's recipe.

1. Place the pork in a large bowl and add all other ingredients, mixing thoroughly by hand.
2. Cover and allow to sit in refrigerator for several hours.
3. If the chorizo is not going to be used immediately, pack the uncooked mixture in a well-covered storage container and refrigerate. It will keep for two weeks.

Cabbage with Juniper Berries

SERVES 4 TO 6

1 small savoy cabbage
(about 1 1/2 pounds)

Salt and freshly ground
black pepper to taste

1 tablespoon butter

1 leek, white part
with a little green,
cut in julienne strips

10 juniper berries,
bruised

1/2 cup heavy cream

Deborah Madison, author of *The Greens Cookbook* (Bantam, 1987) and *The Savory Way* (Bantam, 1990), teaches at the Cooking School as a guest chef. Noted for her vegetarian cooking, Deborah has started incorporating into her recipes foods indigenous to the Southwest since moving to Santa Fe five years ago. The following recipe uses juniper berries, which grow abundantly on the hills surrounding Santa Fe.

1. Quarter the cabbage, remove the core and any wilted leaves, and cut into wide ribbons or squares.
2. Bring a pot of water to a boil, add cabbage and salt to taste, and cook 4 minutes. Drain, rinse with cool water, and press out excess moisture by hand.
3. Melt the butter and add leeks, juniper berries, and a tablespoon of water. Cook over medium heat for 3 to 4 minutes. Add the cabbage and cream. Adjust salt, if needed. Cover the pan and cook over low heat until the cabbage has absorbed the cream, 15 to 20 minutes. Taste again for salt and season with plenty of pepper.

Calabacitas with Corn and Tomatoes

SERVES 8

2 tablespoons butter

2 tablespoons olive oil

1 cup finely chopped onion

2 teaspoons minced garlic

2 1/2 cups diced yellow summer squash

2 1/2 cups diced zucchini squash

3/4 cup (1 bunch) finely chopped green onions

1 cup fresh or frozen corn kernels

1/2 cup mild roasted, peeled, and chopped green chile

1/2 cup hot roasted, peeled, and chopped green chile

1 cup diced ripe Roma (Italian plum) tomatoes

1/2 cup (packed) coarsely chopped fresh cilantro

Salt to taste

Calabacitas (squash) is popular because it is so versatile. It can be as simple or elegant as the occasion demands. In many Santa Fe homes, calabacitas is frequently made into a one-dish casserole by adding chicken or beef and baking. The following recipe for a side dish of mixed vegetables can be served whenever a lively vegetable dish is called for.

1. Heat the butter and olive oil in a large skillet and sauté the onion until softened, about 4 minutes. Add the garlic and sauté 2 minutes.
2. Add the diced squash and sauté for about 5 minutes, until softened. Add the green onion, corn, and green chile and sauté for 3 minutes. Stir in the diced tomato and cilantro and heat through. Season with salt to taste and serve.

VARIATIONS:

For a different flavor, add any of these optional ingredients during the last five minutes of simmering:
1/2 cup chicken stock
1/2 cup heavy cream
grated Jack or cheddar cheese
ground canela

CALABACITAS IN HISTORY

For more than 2,000 years squash, corn, and beans have composed the triad of foods that has supported life in the great Pueblo Indian cultures of the Southwest. Corn and beans supplied the essential proteins and carbohydrates, and squash, through its seeds rich in oil, put fat into the diets of the early New Mexican people. The belief that squash was sacred is well-illustrated by the squash motifs that appear on ancient pottery and jewelry of the Southwest. Archaeological studies tell us that squash was probably the oldest cultivated staple of Mesoamerica, having been grown at least 7,500 years ago in Mexico.

Chicos con Carne

YIELD: 8 TO 10 SERVINGS

1 pound beef stew meat or pork, or 1/2 pound of each

2 to 3 cups chicos

1/4 cup diced onion

1 garlic clove, minced

1 bay leaf

Salt and freshly ground black pepper to taste

VARIATION:

You can use chicken stock in place of water for a richer tasting chico dish.

Deloris Casados of Rancho Casados contributed this recipe for chicos. I love chicos, and my favorite come from Morairity, which is in central New Mexico. The corn in this area is especially sweet. If you should visit the Santa Fe Farmer's Market, you will see a large trailer loaded with fresh sweet corn from Morairity. They sell out quickly, so be sure to arrive early if you want to buy some. The Cooking School purchases as many chicos as we can from Morairity. However, they are hard to come by because almost all of the corn grown is sold as fresh ears.

1. Brown the meat in a stew pot.
2. Add the chicos, onion, garlic, and bay leaf and water to cover. Season with salt and pepper. Cook for about 2 hours, or until the meat is well done.
3. Chicos may also be cooked along with pinto beans in place of meat. Use 2 to 3 cups of beans to each cup of chicos.

CHICOS

Chico, which means small in Spanish, is corn that has been partially shucked, roasted on the cob, and dried. This results in a chewy corn kernel. Traditionally, roasting takes place in horno ovens, which are beehive-shaped ovens made of adobe. To roast chicos in the horno ovens, fires are built in the ovens for several hours until they reach a very high temperature. The coals and ash of the fire are removed and the cobs of corn are thrown in the horno ovens along with small amounts of water to create steam. The openings to the ovens are then sealed with adobe bricks and mud plaster and the corn is allowed to roast for approximately 12 hours. Next, the adobe bricks and mud are dismantled and the cobs of corn removed. The cobs are then allowed to dry on drying racks or by hanging. When the corn is completely dry (after approximately 7 days, depending on the weather), the kernels are removed from the cob and sorted. Chicos are not common outside the Southwest, but they are an authentic part of Santa Fe cooking.

Chicos with Calabacitas

Corn and squash have both been staples of the Southwestern diet for many years. The combination is nutritious as well as attractive. This particular recipe has been especially well liked in the Southwest Vegetarian class at the Cooking School.

YIELD:
1 CUP COOKED CHICOS

CHICOS:

1/3 cup chicos

3 cups water

1. Bring the chicos and water to a boil and reduce the heat to a simmer. Cook for about 90 minutes, until the chicos have softened and are plump and chewy. Drain.

CALABACITAS:

1 tablespoon butter

1 tablespoon olive oil

1 cup finely chopped onion

1 teaspoon minced garlic

2 cups cubed yellow summer squash

2 cups cubed zucchini squash

1/2 cup thinly sliced green onions

1/2 cup roasted, chopped green chile, hot or mild

1 teaspoon salt, or to taste

1/2 cup seeded and diced ripe tomato

1/3 cup coarsely chopped fresh cilantro

1. Heat butter and olive oil in a large skillet over medium high. Sauté onion for about 2 minutes. Add garlic and continue cooking for 2 minutes, stirring frequently.

2. Add yellow and green squash and cook for 4 minutes. Add green onions, chicos, and chile and cook for 2 minutes. Season with salt and add tomato and cilantro. Cook for 2 minutes and serve.

Chile-Glazed Bacon

SERVES 6

1/2 pound sliced slab bacon

1/4 cup Santa Fe Olé red-chile honey (recipe for honey follows)

3 tablespoons jalapeño mustard (recipe follows)

1 tablespoon apple cider vinegar

RED CHILE HONEY:

Mix 1 cup honey with 1 tablespoon red chile powder and 1/4 teaspoon each ground cumin and garlic salt. Combine all ingredients in a small saucepan on low heat and cook for 1 minute, stirring constantly.

JALAPEÑO MUSTARD:

Combine 1 cup yellow mustard with 2 minced jalapeño peppers (stems removed) and 1/2 tea-spoon turmeric. Blend well and allow to sit for at least 1 hour to develop full flavors.

There is nothing like the aromas of bacon cooking and coffee brewing to start off the day. This version of chile-glazed bacon is a sure winner. It is part of our Southwest Breakfast class, which was designed by Cheryl Alters Jamison. The bacon from Embudo Station Smokehouse is incredibly good and is available by mail (see source list on page 160). Used as a baste during the last few minutes of cooking, the spicy chile glaze also does wonderful things for baked winter squash, roasted or grilled poultry, and pork tenderloins.

1. Preheat the oven to 350 degrees.
2. Arrange the bacon in a single layer on a baking sheet with sides. Bake about 10 minutes and pour off rendered fat.
3. Mix the remaining ingredients together and brush the bacon with the mixture. Return the bacon to the oven and bake about 4 minutes. Turn the bacon over, brush the bacon with the mixture again, and return the tray to the oven for another 4 minutes, until the bacon is medium brown and crispy. Serve hot.

EMBUDO STATION

At the School, we slice our own bacon off of a slab which has been smoked at Embudo Station, a picturesque dining facility/smoke house/microbrewery located on the banks of the Rio Grande River. Embudo Station was on the Chile Line, a railroad constructed in 1880 which promoted the trade of chiles from northern New Mexico for potatoes grown in southern Colorado. On our culinary tour of Embudo Station, we not only have lunch and sample the beer from the microbrewery, but we enjoy a tour and learning about the historical background of the station.

2 ~ ~ ~ canola or
vegetable ~.

1 1/2 cups long grain
white rice

1 cup chopped
white onion

1 teaspoon minced garlic

1 1/4 cups canned
crushed tomatoes

1 tablespoon pure
ground red chile, or
more to taste

1 teaspoon salt

1 3/4 cups water

Mexican Rice

A light recipe with an amazing depth of flavor, this is a joy to prepare because it is virtually foolproof.

1. Heat the oil in a saucepan over medium-high heat and sauté the rice until it is opaque and golden, about 5 to 7 minutes.
2. Add the onions and garlic and sauté for 2 minutes. Stir in the tomatoes, chile, salt, and water, and bring the mixture to a boil. Reduce the heat to low, cover, and simmer about 30 minutes, or until the water has been absorbed.
3. Turn off the heat, uncover the rice, and stir to incorporate the added ingredients. Replace the lid and let the rice steam for an additional 10 to 15 minutes. Fluff the rice with a fork and serve.

VARIATIONS:

You may stir in any or all of the following ingredients while the rice is steaming, about 5 minutes before serving:
3/4 cup frozen baby peas, thawed to room temperature
3/4 cup fresh corn kernels, or frozen, thawed
1/2 cup finely diced roasted, seeded, peeled fresh poblano chile

Parmesan-Cilantro Potatoes

YIELD: 6 SERVINGS

3 Russet baking potatoes, peeled and cut in half lengthwise

1 cup chicken stock

Salt and freshly ground black pepper to taste

1 cup slivered onion

1/2 cup grated Parmesan cheese

3 tablespoons melted butter

2 tablespoons coarsely chopped fresh cilantro

1. Preheat the oven to 350 degrees.
2. With a small, sharp knife, make diagonal incisions in each potato half to within 1/4-inch of the bottom, being careful not to cut all the way through the potato. Place the potatoes in a Pyrex baking dish, flat-side down. Add the chicken stock and sprinkle with salt, pepper, onions, and cheese. Drizzle the potatoes with melted butter and bake for about 1 hour, or until they are cooked through. Sprinkle each serving with fresh cilantro.

Pecan-Stuffed Acorn Squash

SERVES 8

2 medium acorn squash, quartered and seeded

Salt and freshly ground pepper to taste

1/3 cup coarsely chopped pecans

1 1/2 teaspoons ground cumin seed

1/3 cup brown sugar

2 tablespoons melted butter

1 tablespoon finely chopped fresh parsley

Certain species of Cucurbita, or the genus comprising pumpkins, squash, and gourds, have been the mainstays of the diets of people on this continent as far back as pre-Columbian times. Acorn squash is one of the better-keeping winter varieties and is excellent when baked and embellished with spices and nuts. Stored in the refrigerator, acorn squash will keep for a month or more.

1. Preheat the oven to 350 degrees.
2. Place the quartered squash in a Pyrex baking dish and season with salt, pepper. Add water to a depth of about 1/2-inch. Cover with foil and bake the squash about 45 minutes, or until soft.
3. Combine the remaining ingredients in a small bowl and mix thoroughly. Remove the foil from the squash and place some of the stuffing in the well of each squash. Bake 5 minutes more. Serve.

Pinto Beans with Chile

SERVES 8

1 pound pinto beans
(2 1/3 cups), picked over
for dirt and stones

2 tablespoons peanut oil
or vegetable oil

1 1/4 cups diced onion

1 tablespoon minced
garlic

4 cups chicken broth or
water, or a combination
of the two

2 small bay leaves

1 1/2 teaspoons dried
Mexican oregano

1 1/2 teaspoons dried
epazote

1/2 teaspoon ground
cumin seed

1/2 teaspoon ground
coriander seed

1 dried chipotle chile

1 1/2 teaspoons juice
from a can of chipotle
chiles in adobo sauce
(optional)

1 teaspoon salt, or to
taste

VARIATION:

Frequently, recipes for
pinto beans include a
ham hock, salt pork, or
bacon. If this idea sounds
appealing, add 1 ham
hock, whole, or 2 slices
of salt pork or bacon,
diced, while sautéing the
onion.

Pinto beans, like posole, are served with almost every New Mexican meal. You see them in breakfast burritos, and they are served as a side dish with both lunch and dinner. The beans are so named because of their spotted appearance, and they have been grown in New Mexico for centuries. They provide an excellent source of iron and protein at a very low cost. We cook beans frequently at the Cooking School. However, there is no consensus amongst the chefs on how to cook them. Some say soak the beans, and some say don't. Some are in favor of discarding the cooking water and others are not. If you are most concerned with flavor, don't soak the beans, and don't discard the water. However, there are other considerations. As I am sure you know, beans have an anti-social characteristic. To help with this, cook the beans until they are slightly soft, discard the water, and add the herb epazote. I suggest you experiment with beans, as some people are more susceptible to the gas-producing qualities of beans. If you are not, keep the water the beans were cooked in because it imparts a rich flavor.

1. Place the beans in a 6-quart pot, cover with cold water by 3 inches, and bring to a boil. Reduce the heat and simmer the beans for 2 to 3 hours, until the beans begin to soften. Drain the beans and rinse well.
2. Heat the oil in a 6-quart pot over medium-high heat and sauté the onions until golden. Add the garlic and cook for 1 minute.
3. Add the beans, broth, bay leaves, oregano, epazote, cumin, coriander, and dried chile and bring to a boil. Reduce the heat and simmer for approximately 1 hour, stirring frequently. Add more liquid if needed.
4. When the beans are creamy, add the optional canned chipotle chile juice, if desired, and the salt and cook 15 minutes more. The beans should have enough liquid to stir easily.

COOKING BEANS

Do not add salt or any ingredients which contain acid, such as vinegar, citrus juice, or tomatoes to beans until they have softened because it inhibits the cooking process and the beans will be tough.

WHAT IS EPAZOTE?

Epazote (ehp-ah-zoh-teh) is a classic seasoning for beans, and it is also used to make beans more socially acceptable because of its anti-flatulent qualities. This pungent, annual herb grows wild in Mexico and the United States. Used dried or fresh, there is no substitute for its distinctive and incomparable flavor. Known also as wormseed and goosefoot, it is considered a weed in many countries, but it is almost a prerequisite for a pot of beans in Hispanic cooking.

ORGANIC GARDENING

David Rigsby is a certified organic farmer from Nirvana Mañana Acres, located on the banks of the Rio Grande River near Embudo. A large part of his farming effort is geared toward growing beautiful, but hard to grow heirloom beans. Varieties such as Taos Kiva, Rams Horn, Calipso, and White Aztec, with their unusual shapes and colors, are a few of the heirloom beans he grows. Being a certified organic farmer, David strives to grow soil rich in microorganisms and humus. He views the soil as the crop, and the produce as the byproduct.

According to David, to be an organic farmer requires conviction. Organic farmers often trade a lower crop yield for increased nutritional value in the crop they produce. The availability of minerals from plot to plot encourages and demands the farmer's or backyard gardener's sensitivity to growing the appropriate plant rather than striving to make all land the same by the application of artificial fertilizers, pesticides, and herbicides. Organic gardening requires a big time investment in hand weeding, spreading manure, planting cover crops, and rotating crops.

Frijoles Refritos

SERVES 6

4 tablespoons vegetable oil or lard

3/4 cup finely chopped onion

2 teaspoons minced garlic

3 cups well-cooked pinto beans, drained, and reserved cooking liquid

2 chiles chipotles from a can of Chiles Chipotles in Adobo Sauce, chopped

Salt to taste

These earthy yet flavorful beans can be even further enhanced by topping with grated cheese, chopped roasted green chiles, salsa fresca, or cooked and crumbled chorizo or bacon. Some version of this recipe has been used at the School since it opened. Each chef has altered the basic bean recipe to his or her liking, and I encourage you to do the same.

1. Heat the oil in a large skillet and sauté onion until softened, about 4 minutes. Add the garlic and sauté 2 minutes.

2. Add beans and chipotles, and mash the mixture with a bean masher or the back of a large spoon, adding the reserved bean cooking liquid or water until a thick paste is formed. You can also use a food processor to "mash" the beans. To do this, transfer about 3/4 of the bean mixture to a food processor and pulse until mixture is coarsely pureed. Return the beans to the pan. Continue to cook, stirring, until heated through. If the beans seem too dry, add a little more liquid. Salt to taste. Serve as a side dish or spread on fresh flour tortillas to make burritos.

USING LARD

According to the USDA, lard has less than half the cholesterol of butter and is one of the less-saturated animal fats. It also has a lot of oleic acid, the most important monounsaturated fatty acid. Substituting oils and shortenings for lard changes a dish considerably because each type of fat holds and blends other flavors in its own way.

Nirvana Mañana Beans

YIELD: APPROXIMATELY 2 CUPS

1/4 pound (1/2 cup) heirloom beans

3 cups water

1/8 teaspoon each ground cumin & black pepper

1/4 teaspoon each Italian seasoning and minced garlic

1/2 teaspoon salt

1/2 onion, grated or diced

1 teaspoon bacon grease or meat drippings to taste (optional)

1. Soak beans overnight. Discard water and add three cups water. Add rest of ingredients except salt.

2. Cook 2 to 3 hours over low heat until beans are soft. Check frequently, adding water if necessary add salt.

Fried Potatoes with Red Chile Sauce

SERVES 6

2 pounds red- or white-skinned potatoes

Canola or vegetable oil for frying

1 1/2 cups finely chopped onion

2 teaspoons minced garlic

1 to 1 1/2 cups Red Chile Sauce (see recipe on page 118)

1 cup grated mild cheddar cheese

Salt to taste

Sour cream and fresh cilantro for garnish

This spicy version of fried potatoes, which is part of the Southwest Breakfast class, also makes a tasty filling for burritos. Fill warm flour tortillas with several heaping spoonfuls of potatoes. Roll up. Serve with extra red chile sauce on the side.

1. Cut the potatoes into 1/2-inch cubes. Heat 1/2 inch of oil in a large skillet over medium-high heat. Add the onion and sauté for 2 minutes. Add the garlic and sauté for 2 minutes.
2. Add the potatoes, reduce the heat to medium, and cook, stirring frequently, until the potatoes are crisp on the outside and soft on the inside.
3. Add the chile sauce and cheese, and season with salt to taste. Serve garnished with a dollop of sour cream and freshly chopped cilantro.

Chipotle Polenta

3 cups chicken stock

1 tablespoon butter

1 cup polenta

1 to 2 tablespoons juice from a can of Chipotle Chiles in Adobo Sauce

1 teaspoon salt

The tantalizing, smoky flavor of the chipotle chile distinguishes this polenta. Polenta is a cornmeal dish typically served in Italy, but it adapts extremely well to Southwestern cuisine.

1. In a medium saucepan, bring the chicken stock to a boil. Add the butter and slowly pour in the polenta, whisking as you pour. Reduce the heat to low and whisk frequently. Add the chipotle liquid and salt and continue whisking until the polenta is thick, about 10 to 15 minutes.
2. Spray an 8-inch square baking dish with vegetable cooking spray and pour the polenta into the dish, flattening it to form a smooth surface. Let it stand about 20 minutes, or until firm. At this point you can cut the polenta into any shape you like for serving.
3. When ready to use, preheat the oven to 350 degrees and return the polenta to the oven to heat through.

CANOLA OIL

Canola oil, which is pressed from rapeseed, possesses several properties that make it an ideal choice for general cooking needs at the Cooking School. Canola oil is used in dishes which require a relatively bland oil flavor that will allow the natural flavors of the foods to come through. Canola also has a high smoking point, which is necessary in oils that are used for frying. Health benefits lie in its high mono- and polyunsaturated fats and low saturated fats and in the fact that you don't need to use much. "Less is more" proves to be true when using high-quality oils for cooking.

Posole

Posole is served as a side dish in restaurants with most New Mexican dishes. It is as common in New Mexico as potatoes are in other parts of the country. The recipes and variations for posole are endless. If you would like to serve it as an entree, add pork. For special occasions during the holiday season and feast days on pueblos, cooks in New Mexico serve posole with pork added.

1. Put the posole in a 6-quart pot and cover with cold water by 3 inches. Bring to a boil, reduce the heat, and simmer for 2 to 3 hours, adding water as needed, until the kernels have softened and begun to burst.
2. Drain the posole and rinse well.
3. Heat the oil in a 6-quart pot and sauté the onions until golden. Add the garlic and sauté for 1 minute. Add the posole, dried chiles, and broth and bring to a boil. Reduce the heat and simmer for 30 minutes.
4. Add the salt and continue cooking for 30 minutes. Stir in the cilantro, taste, and adjust seasonings. Serve.

VARIATION:

Omit the fresh cilantro and add 2 teaspoons of dried Mexican oregano with the posole, chiles, and broth. Two teaspoons of azafran can be added at the same point; this gives the posole a lovely golden color and an interesting aroma and flavor. You could also serve bowls of red or green chile sauce on the side to flavor the posole further. Garnishes can include shredded lettuce or cabbage, thinly sliced radishes, and lime wedges.

**SERVES 8
AS A MAIN COURSE,
10 TO 12 AS A SIDE DISH**

2 pounds (4 3/4 cups) posole, picked over for any dirt or stones

1/4 cup vegetable oil

2 1/2 cups chopped onion

2 tablespoons minced garlic

1 ounce New Mexican dried red chile pods (4 to 5 pods) stemmed, with the seeds removed

8 cups chicken broth

2 teaspoons salt, to taste

1 cup coarsely chopped cilantro

AZAFRAN

Azafran is a safflower, or Mexican saffron orange thistle, not the true, expensive stigmas of the saffron crocus. Use it for flavoring, as in posole, and as a nice color additive.

POSOLE

The Mayas, Aztecs, and native North Americans who boiled corn in water mixed with ashes were probably unaware that they were increasing the nutrient value of their corn. According to modern science, the ash allows the release of chemically bound niacin and renders amino acids more readily available to the body. Today, posole is processed in a fashion similar to the Mayan and Aztec method. Dry corn kernels are boiled in a hydrate-lime solution for approximately one hour or until the hulls come off. They are then rinsed and washed thoroughly to remove the lime solution. The kernels are then placed on drying racks and turned to prevent molding. When ground, posole is called masa harina and is used to make corn tortillas, tamale dough, and corn chips. It is available in many grocery stores throughout the country.

Red Chile Mashed Potatoes

SERVES 6

1 head garlic

2 teaspoons olive oil

1 tablespoon white wine (optional)

4 russet or Yukon Gold potatoes

1 tablespoon butter

3/4 cup milk (lowfat or whole)

1/4 cup sour cream (reduced fat or regular)

2 tablespoons New Mexican ground red chile

1 to 2 teaspoons salt

Freshly ground black pepper to taste

Chile in almost everything from breakfast foods to desserts is common in Santa Fe. Mashed potatoes are no exception. Visiting guest chef Jacqueline Higuera McMahan contributed this hard-to-resist recipe.

1. Place the garlic on a square of foil and drizzle with olive oil and wine. Wrap the garlic tightly and roast in a 350 degree oven for 45 minutes, or until soft. Using the tip of a sharp paring knife, lift out each clove.
2. Peel the potatoes and place in a pot of boiling, salted water. Cook 30 minutes, or until very tender but not falling apart. Drain.
3. Put the potatoes in a mixer fitted with the whisk attachment. Break up the potatoes with a fork. With the mixer going, slowly add the butter, milk, sour cream, red chile, and roasted garlic to taste. Add salt and pepper to taste and continue beating for a couple of minutes. Garnish with a dusting of chile powder and chopped cilantro. Serve immediately.

VARIATION:

For an even spicier dish, you can also add 1/2 cup roasted, peeled, chopped green chile.

Red Chile Roasted Potatoes

SERVES 6

3 tablespoons vegetable oil

1 cup finely chopped onion

24 ounces Idaho potatoes, cut in 1/2-inch cubes

2 tablespoons pure ground chile

Salt to taste

2 tablespoons coarsely chopped fresh cilantro

1. Preheat the oven to 350 degrees.
2. Heat the oil in a medium skillet oven medium-high heat. Add the onion and cook for 4 minutes, or until softened.
3. Place the potatoes in a bowl and toss with the cooked onion. Add the chile and salt, stirring to combine thoroughly. Scrape the mixture into an 8-inch-square baking pan and bake for 40 minutes, until the potatoes are golden and cooked through. Sprinkle with fresh cilantro and serve.

Southwestern Scalloped Potatoes with Green Chile and Cheese

SERVES 6 TO 8

1 1/2 pounds new potatoes, well scrubbed and thinly sliced

3/4 to 1 cup heavy cream

3/4 to 1 cup chopped roasted green chiles, hot or mild, depending on taste

3/4 to 1 cup grated Monterey Jack or cheddar cheese

1/2 cup diced red onion

4 tablespoons butter

2 teaspoons salt, or to taste

1 teaspoon freshly ground canela

1. Preheat oven to 350 degrees.
2. Lightly oil a 9 x 12-inch baking dish.
3. Place a thin layer of potatoes in the baking dish and top with 1/4 cup cream. Top with chile, cheese, onion, butter, and sprinklings of salt and canela. Repeat layers. Bake 40 to 50 minutes, or until the potatoes are soft and the top is golden.

VARIATION:

Substituting lowfat buttermilk for the heavy cream reduces the calories and the fat, while lending a pleasing, tangy flavor.

Summer Squash Stuffed with Cheese and Peppers

SERVES 6

4 medium yellow summer squash, about 5 to 6 ounces each

2 tablespoons vegetable oil or butter

1/2 cup finely chopped onion

1 teaspoon minced garlic

1/3 cup red bell pepper

1/3 cup yellow bell pepper

1 to 2 tablespoons roasted, chopped green chile

1 tablespoon chopped parsley

1/2 teaspoon salt

1 cup grated cheddar cheese

1. Preheat the oven to 350 degrees.
2. Cut three of the squash in half and scoop out the seeds. Dice the fourth squash into in 1/4-inch cubes and set aside.
3. In a medium skillet, heat the oil over medium heat. Add the onion and cook until soft, about 3 minutes. Add the garlic and cook 1 minute more.
4. Add the diced squash, bell peppers, and green chile and cook until the squash is tender, about 4 minutes. Stir in the parsley and season with salt.
5. Cool the mixture slightly and spoon into the squash halves. Place the stuffed squash on a sheet pan and bake for 15 minutes. Sprinkle the squash with grated cheese and return to the oven for 5 minutes more. Serve.

Julienne of Summer Squash, Carrots, and Red Peppers

SERVES 6

2 tablespoons olive oil

2 tablespoons butter

4 carrots, julienned

2 zucchini, julienned

2 yellow squash, julienned

1 red bell pepper cut into thin strips

2 teaspoons Mexican oregano

2 tablespoons minced fresh parsley

Salt and freshly ground black pepper to taste

This highly flavored dish has evolved from the Spanish sofrito, an ancient flavoring mixture made of sautéed vegetables, fat, and herbs or spices. By bringing the vegetables and fat to a higher temperature than that of boiling water, the flavors are boldly enriched and intensified.

1. Heat the olive oil and butter in a sauté pan over medium-high heat. Sauté the carrots for 2 minutes. Add the zucchini, yellow squash, and bell pepper and sauté for about 5 minutes, tossing the ingredients thoroughly as they cook.
2. Add the oregano, parsley, salt, and pepper and combine thoroughly. Serve immediately.

Pumpkin Cheesecake

SWEET ENDINGS:

Southwestern Desserts

This chapter offers a variety of delicious recipes for indulging one's passion for sweets. Many of the traditional recipes, such as the Capirotada (bread pudding) have a lengthy history in New Mexico. Other recipes, such as the Pumpkin Cheesecake and Berry-Pecan Flan, reflect the more contemporary uses of indigenous products.

Apricot Empanaditas

MAKES 4 DOZEN BITE-SIZED EMPANADITAS

PASTRY:

2 cups flour

1/2 teaspoon salt

1 1/2 sticks unsalted butter

1/4 cup vegetable shortening

6 ounces cream cheese, at room temperature

FILLING:

1 1/4 cups dried apricots

1/2 cup apricot or pineapple preserves

3 tablespoons triple sec

2 tablespoons sugar

1/4 cup dry bread crumbs

GLAZE:

1 egg

1 tablespoon water

Granulated sugar

We have used this recipe a number of times at the School for holiday classes and welcome receptions for the culinary tours. You truly cannot eat just one of these. Empanaditas are savory or sweet turnovers traditionally made with a lard crust and then deep-fried. This baked version is adapted for more contemporary tastes.*

1. Combine the flour and salt in the workbowl of a food processor. Scatter pieces of the butter, shortening, and cream cheese over the flour and process briefly until a soft dough forms. This can be done in a bowl with a pastry blender or 2 forks as well.
2. Divide the dough into 2 balls. Wrap each ball in plastic and refrigerate at least 2 hours. The dough can be prepared a day ahead.
3. Chop the apricots. Cover them with water in a saucepan and simmer until soft, about 20 minutes. Add the preserves, triple sec, and sugar and continue to simmer until thick, another 10 minutes or so. Stir in the bread crumbs.
4. Roll out each ball of the chilled dough on a floured surface to about 1/8-inch in thickness. Cut the dough into rounds with a biscuit or cookie cutter. Top each round with a dollop of filling. Fold the round in half, pinch the edges to seal the empanadita, and then crimp with a fork.
5. Combine the egg with the water to glaze each empanadita. Sprinkle lightly with sugar. Bake at 375 degrees for 20 minutes. (If you find the filling is oozing out of the pastry when baking, use less filling per empanada.) Serve warm or at room temperature.

*A version of this superb dessert will appear in Bill and Cheryl Alters Jamisons' newest cookbook, *The Border Cookbook,* published by Harvard Common Press.

Spiced Bananas with Rum

SERVES 6

3 large bananas or 6 small ones

1/4 cup unsalted butter

1/3 cup brown sugar, packed

1/4 cup dark rum

1/2 teaspoon Santa Fe Seasons Sweet Spice (See Note)

1 teaspoon Mexican vanilla

Unsweetened whipped cream or vanilla ice cream

This Southwest variation on bananas foster is part of our Vegetarian class. It is important that the bananas be ripe but not overly ripe. This dessert is perfect for those times when you have unexpected dinner guests and need a quick and easy finale.

1. Peel the bananas and cut them in half lengthwise.
2. Heat the butter in a large skillet over medium. Add the bananas, cut sides down, and lightly brown them on both sides. Add the sugar, rum, Sweet Spice, and vanilla. Spoon this mixture over the bananas and serve with a dollop of whipped cream or vanilla ice cream.

NOTE:

If you do not have Santa Fe Seasons Sweet Spice, substitute a blend of cinnamon or canela, allspice, nutmeg, and cloves.

Tequila Cream Sauce Parfait

YIELD: 6 SERVINGS

1 stick (4 ounces) unsalted butter

4 egg yolks

2 tablespoons water

5 tablespoons powdered sugar

2 teaspoons vanilla

1/4 to 1/3 cup gold tequila, to taste

1 cup heavy cream, chilled

Fresh pineapple, strawberries, kiwis, bananas, raspberries, blueberries, or any other available fresh fruit

1. Melt the butter.
2. Bring an inch of water to a low boil in the bottom of a large saucepan or bain-marie.
3. Whisk together the egg yolks and 2 tablespoons of water in a stainless steel bowl that will fit securely into the top of the saucepan or whisk the yolks and water together in the top of the bain-marie. Fit the bowl into the top of the saucepan and whisk the yolk mixture until stiff.
4. Remove the bowl from the pan and slowly pour the melted butter into the yolks, whisking constantly, until the butter is absorbed into the yolks. Whisk in the sugar, vanilla, and tequila. Whip the cream until fairly stiff and fold it into the egg mixture until smooth. Layer the sauce with the fresh fruit in chilled wine glasses or parfait glasses.

Berry-Pecan Flan

This is a good dessert after a hot and spicy meal as the cream cheese diminishes any heat lingering in the mouth. You can use almost any type of berry. However, my favorite are raspberries grown locally in the village of Mora. If you live in New Mexico or are visiting in the early fall, it is worth the scenic drive to Mora to purchase freshly picked raspberries in season.

CRUST:

3/4 cup unsalted butter, softened

1/2 cup powdered sugar

1 1/2 cups flour

1/4 cup ground pecans

1. Preheat oven to 325 degrees.
2. Mix all ingredients and pat into greased flan pan.
3. Bake 10 to 12 minutes until lightly browned. Cool.

FILLING:

8 ounces cream cheese, softened

1/2 cup sugar

1 teaspoon Mexican vanilla

1. Mix all ingredients together and spread on the bottom of the cooled flan shell.

TOPPING:

1/2 pint strawberries, sliced, or whole raspberries

1/2 cup pecan halves

1. Arrange decoratively on top of cream cheese spread, covering evenly.

SAUCE:

1 cup cranberry juice (unsweetened)

2 tablespoons cornstarch

1 teaspoon lemon juice

1/2 cup sugar

1 cup Salmon Ranch raspberry jam

1. Combine all ingredients in a small, heavy saucepan and cook over low heat, stirring constantly, for about 2 minutes. Sauce will thicken slightly.
2. Cool to room temperature and spread over the fruit and pecans on the flan.
3. Chill before serving.

SALMON RANCH RASPBERRY JAM

Salmon Ranch Raspberry Jam is made with raspberries grown high in the Sangre de Cristo mountains of northern New Mexico. The jam is as good as homemade raspberry jam. The pure flavor of the fruit predominates. If it is not available, substitute the highest quality raspberry jam you can find.

Biscochitos

MAKES 4 TO 5 DOZEN
COOKIES

1 pound (2 cups) lard,
vegetable shortening, or
butter

1 1/2 cups sugar

2 eggs

2 teaspoons toasted anise
seeds

6 cups flour

3 teaspoons
baking powder

1 teaspoon salt

1/2 cup brandy

TOPPING:

1/2 cup sugar

1 teaspoon cinnamon

This delicious shortbread-like cookie is associated with special occasions in New Mexico such as weddings, baptisms, and of course, Christmas. I highly recommend using lard rather than vegetable oil in this recipe. The flakiness and flavor that the lard imparts cannot be achieved using vegetable oil. Some cooks substitute butter or margarine, with both a loss of flavor and a gain in cholesterol, as butter contains twice as much cholesterol as lard.

1. Preheat the oven to 350 degrees.
2. Cream the shortening. Add sugar, eggs, and anise seeds and cream again. Mix dry ingredients separately and combine with the shortening mixture. Add the brandy and mix thoroughly.
3. Roll the dough out on a floured surface and cut into desired shapes. Sprinkle the cookie shapes with the sugar-cinnamon mixture and bake for 12 to 15 minutes until lightly browned.

IT'S THE STATE COOKIE!

In 1989, the New Mexico state legislature made biscochitos the New Mexico State Cookie. Thus New Mexico became the first state to have an official state cookie, indicating the importance that New Mexico places on food.

ANISE SEED

Anise seeds were introduced in the early 1800s by Spanish priests, who brought few precious spices from Spain when they came to New Mexico via Mexico's Chihuahua Trail. The seed has a licorice flavor and is used in both sweet and savory dishes.

Blue Cornmeal Shortcakes

**YIELD: 12 SHORTCAKES
(2 INCHES IN DIAMETER)**

3 cups cake flour

1/2 cup blue cornmeal

3 tablespoons sugar

1 1/2 tablespoons
baking powder

3/4 teaspoon coarse salt

1 teaspoon freshly
ground coriander seed

6 ounces unsalted butter,
chilled and cubed

1 1/4 cups heavy cream

Add some fruit and whipped cream to these incredibly delicious shortcakes, and you have a real crowd pleaser.

1. Preheat the oven to 425 degrees.
2. Mix the dry ingredients thoroughly in the workbowl of a food processor. Add the cubed butter and pulse to a coarse, cornmeal-like consistency. DO NOT OVERPROCESS! If the mixture forms a ball, it's overprocessed.
3. Pour the mixture into a medium bowl and make a well in the center. Add the cream and mix the dough with a fork until it just comes together.
4. Gently roll or pat the dough to a thickness of 3/4 to 1 inch. Cut out circles, and carefully place the shortcakes on lined baking sheets. Sprinkle with cinnamon and granulated sugar and bake for 12 to 15 minutes.

MEXICAN VANILLA

Mexican vanilla, the cured pod of a tropical orchid vine that grows in the humid tropical forests of Vera Cruz, is used in both the pod and liquid forms. The long, thin, black pods contain thousands of minute, flavor-bearing seeds. The pods are slit prior to use and are usually immersed in a simmering liquid, which becomes infused with their lovely, perfumed vanilla flavor. Pods can be washed thoroughly after use and reused.

The liquid vanilla extract from Mexico containing the synthetic flavor coumarin is banned in the United States for health reasons. There are a few companies which import Mexican vanilla beans to the United States for processing. Mexican vanilla, which is approved for sale within the United States, can be ordered through the Cooking School or found in many Hispanic markets.

Capirotada (Sopa)

SERVES 10 TO 12

10 ounces day-old French bread, torn into bite-sized pieces

1/2 cup raisins, or other dried fruit

1/2 cup Madeira, or other sweet wine

2 cups sugar

3 1/2 cups water

5 tablespoons butter

I teaspoon canela or Santa Fe Sweet Spices (see page 147 for substitution recipe)

1 1/2 teaspoons Mexican vanilla

2 ounces (1/2 cup) toasted pecans or piñon nuts

1 cup shredded Monterey Jack or long-horn cheddar cheese

Whipped cream or vanilla ice cream for garnish

For the early northern New Mexican settlers, desserts were usually reserved for special holidays and were intensely sweet and well-flavored with scarce spices. This bread pudding, made without milk and eggs, is traditional in its use of sweet wine, nuts, raisins, and caramel sauce. Any variety of dried fruits, such as apples or apricots, can be used in place of the raisins. Long familiarity has not worn out the appeal of this unique local dessert. The use of cheese in this dessert surprises guests but it never inhibits their enjoyment.

1. Preheat the oven to 350 degrees. Butter a 9 x 12-inch baking dish or pan.
2. Place the bread in the prepared dish and toast in the oven for 20 minutes, or until lightly browned. Soak the raisins in Madeira for 20 minutes and drain, reserving the Madeira.
3. Place the sugar in a heavy saucepan or a large skillet over medium-high heat. Watch the sugar and, when it starts to melt and turn golden around the edges, mash it gently with a large spoon. Stirring will create more lumps and the sugar will take longer to caramelize, so the mashing motion is more effective. Cook the sugar until it turns a deep caramel color. Immediately add the water, being very careful as the hot syrup will bubble and splatter. The caramel will partially solidify but will re-liquify as it reheats.
4. Reduce the heat and add the butter, canela, and vanilla to the caramel syrup, stirring until the butter has melted.
5. Top the toasted bread with nuts and raisins, pouring the reserved Madeira over the mixture. Pour the syrup over the bread and allow it to sit for 5 minutes.
6. Sprinkle the top with grated cheese and additional canela to taste, and bake about 25 minutes, until lightly browned and bubbly. Serve warm with a dollop of whipped cream or vanilla ice cream.

CANELA

Canela, a shaggy-looking, multilayered cinnamon stick, roughly 1/2-inch in diameter, is softer and more easily ground than the harder and darker cinnamon sticks which are commonly found in grocery stores. This soft-stick cinnamon, native to Ceylon (now Sri Lanka), is medium-tan in color, with a flavor that is more lightly perfumed and less pungent than that of the hard cinnamon sticks which are sometimes dipped in flavor enhancing cinnamon oil. Canela is most often used in Mexico and can be ordered from the Cooking School or purchased in Hispanic markets. Cinnamon is an acceptable substitute, but you may want to use slightly less.

Linzertorte El Diablo

SERVES 12 TO 16

PASTRY:

1 1/2 cups
unsalted butter

1 cup extra-fine confec-
tioner's sugar, sifted

1 egg

2 3/4 cups sifted flour

1 1/2 cups ground
hazelnuts or almonds

Pinch of salt

1/2 teaspoon canela

FILLING:

1 cup raspberry jam

1 8-ounce jar Santa Fe
Exotix El Diablo Jam
(if unavailable, substitute
any red chile jam)

1 tablespoon fresh
lemon juice

Powdered sugar

Chef Todd Sanson created this adaptation of a classic linzertorte using jelly from his line of condiments. The El Diablo Jam from Santa Fe Exotix is a spicy, red chile jam which uses brown sugar in place of white. It gives the red chile jam a deeper color and more earthy flavor.

1. Preheat the oven to 375 degrees.
2. Cream the butter with the sugar and egg until light and fluffy. Fold in sifted flour alternating with hazelnuts, salt, and canela. Chill the dough.
3. Roll the dough to 1/4-inch thick and use most of it to cover the bottom of an 11-inch tart pan with a removable bottom.
4. Spread the dough with a mixture of 1 cup raspberry jam and 1 cup Santa Fe Exotix El Diablo Jam and the fresh lemon juice.
5. Roll out the remaining dough, cut it into strips, and form a lattice over the top of the torte.
6. Bake for 40 to 45 minutes. When cooled, remove from the pan and sprinkle with confectioner's sugar.

GROUND NUTS

To grind your own nuts, it is best to use a nut grinder or rotary type of grater and process the nuts until they are the consistency of cornmeal. It is possible to do this in a food processor, but you must be careful not to grind the nuts to a paste. It is also possible to buy finely ground nuts at specialty stores or health food markets.

Fresh Fruit with Tequila-Lime Syrup and Yogurt

SERVES 6

1 cup sugar

2 cups water

2 bunches fresh mint

1/4 cup gold tequila, or to taste

1 to 2 tablespoons fresh lime juice, to taste

1 cup diced fresh pineapple

1 banana, sliced 1/4-inch thick

1/2 cup fresh strawberries, hulled and quartered

1 1/2 cups low-fat yogurt, plain or vanilla

Lusciously light, this dessert will satisfy anyone's sweet tooth. We serve this popular dessert in our Mexican Light class.

1. Place sugar, water, and 1 bunch of mint in a medium saucepan and bring to a boil. Reduce the heat and simmer the mixture for 15 minutes. Add the tequila and continue to simmer 5 minutes more. Turn off the heat and add the lime juice. Cool and strain to remove the mint. This syrup can be refrigerated for later use.

2. Place the pineapple, banana, and strawberries in a bowl. Coarsely chop the leaves from the remaining bunch of mint and sprinkle over the fruit, stirring to combine.

3. Pour the syrup over the fruit and let the mixture stand for 15 to 20 minutes. Serve topped with 1/4 cup of the yogurt.

Piloncillo Baked Apples with Cajeta

SERVES 6

3 large baking apples, cut in half and cored

2 to 2 1/2 ounces cone piloncillo, or 1/4 cup brown sugar

1/3 cup chopped pecans

3 tablespoons butter, softened

1 teaspoon canela or Santa Fe Sweet Spice

1 1/2 cups apple cider or juice

Cajeta (recipe below)

At the School, we use this in our Breakfast class, but it could also serve as a dessert. The cajeta is a rich caramel sauce made with goats milk. Leftovers will keep indefinitely if refrigerated. The cajeta is good on pancakes, waffles, blintzes, ice cream, or fresh fruit. For a milder cajeta, substitute 2 cups of regular cows milk for half of the goat's milk.

1. Preheat the oven to 350 degrees.
2. Arrange the apples in a buttered baking dish.
3. Grate or roughly chop the piloncillo. Combine the piloncillo, pecans, butter, and canela in a small bowl and combine well. Stuff each apple with equal portions of the mixture. Pour cider around the apples and bake for 20 to 30 minutes, until the apples are soft. Serve warm, topped with cajeta.

PILONCILLO

Piloncillo, unrefined sugar, is commonly found in Mexico and is most often seen in small cone shapes. Although dark brown sugar can be used as a substitute for piloncillo, the flavor will be somewhat lessened. Because of its hardness, piloncillo requires grating or chopping before use. It may also be softened in a microwave oven by cooking at a medium heat for approximately 1 to 2 minutes. Piloncillo can be ordered from the Santa Fe School of Cooking or may be found in Hispanic markets.

CAJETA:

1 quart fresh goat's milk or 2 cups evaporated goat's milk combined with 2 cups water

1 cup sugar

1 tablespoon corn syrup

1/4 teaspoon baking soda

1. In a large, heavy saucepan combine all the ingredients except the baking soda and bring to a boil over medium heat.
2. Whisk in the baking soda and reduce the heat to a slow simmer. Cook the mixture for about 1 hour, stirring occasionally initially and more often toward the end. The cajeta will thicken and begin to turn a golden brown. It should be the consistency of melted caramels.

Piñon Nut Pie

1 cup white corn syrup

1 cup dark brown sugar

Pinch of salt

1/3 cup melted butter

1 teaspoon Mexican vanilla

3 whole eggs, slightly beaten

1 heaping cup shelled piñon nuts

1 unbaked pie shell

Whipped cream or vanilla ice cream for garnish

1. Preheat oven to 350 degrees.

2. Combine syrup, sugar, salt, butter, and vanilla and mix well. Add slightly beaten eggs and piñon nuts to mixture and stir. When blended, pour into unbaked pie shell and bake for approximately 55 to 60 minutes until somewhat firm. Top with whipped cream or ice cream.

Piñon Chocolate Torte

SERVES 12

16 ounces semi-sweet or bittersweet chocolate

16 ounces unsalted butter, cut into 1-inch chunks

1 cup Kahlua liqueur

1/2 cup sugar

8 eggs, lightly beaten and strained through a fine sieve

1 tablespoon Mexican vanilla

1 cup roasted piñon nuts

1. Preheat oven to 300 degrees.

2. Place the chocolate, butter, Kahlua, and sugar in the top of a doubleboiler set over barely simmering water. Whisk until smooth. Remove from heat and slowly pour in the eggs. Whisk until well blended. Stir in vanilla and piñon nuts.

3. Pour the mixture into a greased 9-inch round cake pan and bake for 60 to 90 minutes, or until set. Cool in the pan and chill for 4 hours. To remove from the pan, immerse pan briefly to within 1/2-inch of top of pan in a sink of hot water and then invert the cake onto a plate. You may invert again to serve the torte right-side-up.

PIÑON NUTS (PINE NUTS)

The piñon forests of the Southwest produce a food source that dates back to the Anasazi Indians. Records indicate a variety of storage methods and uses for the pine nut. The nuts were eaten raw, roasted, boiled, and ground into a flour. The Navajos mashed the nut into a butter, much like the peanut butter of today. The Southwestern piñon nuts are much richer in flavor and oils than the imported varieties. The nuts are very difficult to harvest and shell and thus command a high price. Commercial harvesting of the piñon forests has declined greatly in past years; however, piñon nut picking remains a part of the New Mexican and Southwestern lifestyle. In the fall, families can be seen in the piñon forests picking the nuts from the ground. The sale of the nuts helps support the traditional life styles of both the Native American and Hispanic cultures.

Polvorones de Naranja

**MAKES ABOUT
36 COOKIES**

1/2 cup unsalted butter

1/2 cup vegetable
shortening

1/2 cup sugar

2 large egg yolks

3 tablespoons orange
juice concentrate,
thawed

1 1/2 tablespoons grated
orange peel

1 teaspoon Mexican
vanilla

4 cups all-purpose flour,
sifted

Powdered sugar for
dusting

Janet Mitchell developed this recipe. Polvorones de Naranja, meaning "orange dusts" in Spanish, are airy cookies similar to the Mexican wedding cookies traditionally served at special occasions. For variety, vanilla and canela are often used in place of the orange flavoring, or ground nuts are added.

1. Preheat oven to 400 degrees.
2. In a large mixing bowl, beat butter and shortening with an electric mixer on medium to high speed, until thoroughly combined and fluffy.
3. Add sugar gradually. Add egg yolks, orange juice concentrate, orange peel, and vanilla. Stir in the flour by hand.
4. Shape the dough into two rolls, 2 1/2-inches in diameter, and wrap each roll in plastic wrap. Refrigerate for 4 to 48 hours.
5. Cut the dough into 1/4-inch slices and place on a lightly greased cookie sheet. Bake for 20 minutes or until cookies are lightly browned around the edges.
6. Cool on a wire rack and dust with the powdered sugar sifted through a fine sieve.

Pumpkin Cheesecake

YIELD:
10 TO 12 SERVINGS

CRUST:

3/4 cup graham cracker crumbs

2 tablespoons sugar

2 tablespoons melted butter

CHEESECAKE:

1 1/2 pounds cream cheese, at room temperature

1 1/2 cups sugar

4 large eggs

3/4 cup canned solid-pack pumpkin

2 teaspoons ground canela, or 1 teaspoon ground cinnamon

1 tablespoon Mexican vanilla

Whipped cream for garnish

The use of pumpkins and squash is centuries old in New Mexico, and this recipe gives a new twist to an old favorite.

1. Preheat the oven to 350 degrees.
2. For the crust, combine the cracker crumbs, sugar, and butter thoroughly. Press the mixture into the bottom of a 9-inch springform pan. Chill in the refrigerator for 15 minutes.
3. In a mixer with a paddle attachment, whip the cream cheese and sugar until light and fluffy.
4. Add the eggs and the pumpkin, and continue beating until the mixture is smooth. Add the canela and vanilla and incorporate thoroughly. Pour the cream cheese mixture into the prepared crust and bake for approximately one hour, or until the cheesecake is set all the way through. Turn off the oven and let the cake sit for 15 minutes. Remove the cake from the oven and chill. Top with whipped cream.

GRINDING SPICES

Two tools to grind spice by hand are the molcajete and the surabachi.

Cooks from Mexico introduced the basalt molcajetes (mortars) and tejolotes (pestles) to New Mexico, where they have long been used for grinding spices and vegetables. The molcajete is a useful piece of equipment for the traditionalist who wants to pulverize small quantities of spices or make a sauce by hand. A blender or an electric spice/coffee grinder will accomplish the same job. The qualities to look for when purchasing a molcajete are weightiness and lack of porosity in the lava rock. Such molcajetes are available for purchase through the Cooking School.

A piece of equipment used daily at the Cooking School to grind spices is the Japanese mortar (surabachi) and wood pestle. It is a high-fired clay bowl with a serrated interior to aid in grinding. Surabachis come in a number of sizes. They are available in Japanese stores and through the Santa Fe School of Cooking.

Santa Fe Coco Palm Tamale

SERVES 6

This recipe was contributed and demonstrated by guest chef John Rivera Sedlar of Abiquiu Restaurant located in Los Angeles and San Francisco. The dessert is Southwestern in appearnce only, and it makes a nice ending to a spicey meal.

ICE CREAM:

2 cups toasted coconut

2 14-ounce cans coconut milk

1 cup milk

3 cups heavy cream

10 egg yolks

1/2 cup sugar

6 corn husks

1. Bring toasted coconut, coconut milk, milk, and cream to a boil. Simmer for about 30 minutes.
2. Add the egg yolks and sugar, return to the heat, and cook, stirring constantly with a wooden spoon, until the mixture coats the spoon. Sieve and let cool. Place in an ice cream machine and process according to manufacturer's directions.

PINEAPPLE SAUCE:

1 ripe pineapple, peeled and cored

1 cup simple syrup

6 tablespoons white rum

1/4 cup corn syrup

1. Purée the pineapple and simple syrup in a food processor. Strain.
2. Add rum and corn syrup and refrigerate.
3. When the ice cream has been spun, place 3/4-cup portions onto 4 x 5-inch plastic sheets and pat the ice cream into rectangles. Dredge each rectangle in shredded coconut and place in the middle of a corn husk. Serve on pineapple sauce.

SIMPLE SYRUP:

1 cup sugar

2 cups water

1. Pour the sugar and the water into a small saucepan and bring to a boil. Reduce the heat to a simmer and continue cooking for 3 to 4 minutes. Cool. Pour into a container, cover, and refrigerate. This syrup will keep for up to 6 months.

Natillas

SERVES 10 TO 12

4 eggs, separated

1/4 cup flour

1 quart heavy cream, divided

3/4 cup sugar, divided

1/8 teaspoon salt

1 1/2 teaspoons Mexican vanilla

Nutmeg, ground canela, or Santa Fe Sweet Spice (see page 147 for substitution recipe)

This dessert is similar to the classic French dessert floating islands, a creamy, egg-based custard with dollops of uncooked meringue garnishing the top. However, here in New Mexico the meringue is folded into the custard and then the custard is stabilized with flour. This method was originally used to extend eggs, which were in short supply. Light adaptations are available for this rich and creamy dessert, but this recipe, developed by Chef Bill Weiland, is so good that I recommend using this rich version and simply eating a smaller portion.

1. Make a paste of the egg yolks, flour, and 1/2 cup of the cream. Add 1/2 cup of the sugar and the salt to the remaining cream and scald in a saucepan. Whisk the scalded cream gradually into the egg mixture and place in a double boiler. Cook slowly, stirring constantly, until the mixture thickens, about 20 minutes.
2. Mix in the vanilla and the let the mixture cool. The recipe can be made ahead to this point.
3. Beat the egg whites with the remaining 1/4 cup of sugar until stiff and shiny but not dry. Fold the egg whites into the cooled custard. Sprinkle with freshly grated nutmeg, ground canela, or Santa Fe Sweet Spice. Serve immediately.

Spiced Winter Pears with Ginger Creme Sauce

YIELD: 6 SERVINGS

6 firm winter pears

1 bottle fruity white wine

1 1/2 cups sugar

1 lemon, peeled and juiced (reserve both peel and juice for use in poaching liquid)

1 teaspoon fennel seeds, lightly crushed

1 vanilla bean, split, or 1 teaspoon Mexican vanilla

2 canela sticks, or 1 cinnamon stick

1/2 teaspoon azafran, or 1/4 teaspoon saffron threads

1. Peel pears, leaving stems on, and core from underneath. Peel lemons, taking care not to cut too deeply into white pith.
2. Combine remaining ingredients in a saucepan just large enough to hold pears upright. Bring to a boil and simmer for 5 minutes.
3. Add pears to simmering poaching syrup and poach for 10 to 15 minutes, or until just tender. Remove pears and allow to cool. Poaching syrup can be saved to poach other fruits, or reduced to make a delicious sauce for other desserts.

GINGER CREME SAUCE:

1/4 cup peeled and finely grated gingerroot

1/3 cup sugar

1/4 cup water

2 cups half-and-half or whole milk

1 vanilla bean, or 1 teaspoon Mexican vanilla

5 egg yolks

1. Place ginger, 2 tablespoons of sugar, and water in a small, heavy-bottomed saucepan. Simmer over very low heat until the syrup becomes thickened, about 5 minutes. Do not allow syrup to caramelize.
2. Add half-and-half and vanilla and bring to a boil. Remove from heat and allow to stand for 1 hour.
3. Beat egg yolks with remaining sugar and whisk together with the half-and-half mixture in the top of a double boiler. Bring an inch of water to a low boil in the bottom of the double boiler. Place the top of the double boiler into the bottom, taking care that the pan is not touching the simmering water.
4. Stir constantly, until slightly thickened, or until mixture reaches 182 degrees on a candy thermometer. Chill thoroughly.
5. To serve, pour about 1/3 cup of creme sauce onto each dessert plate and top with a poached pear. Garnish stem end with a clean pear leaf if desired.

VARIATION:

Janet Mitchell, who created this recipe, suggests reducing the fat by omitting the cream sauce and serving the pear with the reduced poaching liquid and chopped crystalized ginger.

Vanilla Flan

YIELD: 6 SERVINGS

1 1/4 cups sugar, divided

1 cup milk

2 cups heavy cream

2 large eggs

3 large egg yolks

2 teaspoons pure
Mexican vanilla extract

1. Preheat the oven to 325 degrees.

2. Add 1 cup of sugar to a small, dry skillet. Place the skillet over medium-high heat and melt the sugar. As the sugar caramelizes, press the unmelted sugar into the liquefied part with the bottom of a heavy spoon.

3. Reduce the heat to medium and continue cooking until you have a clear, deep-amber liquid. Remove the pan from the heat and immediately pour equal amounts of syrup into six 1/2-cup ramekins, tilting cups to distribute the syrup evenly on the bottoms and sides.

4. In a saucepan over medium heat, combine the milk, cream, and remaining sugar. Heat the mixture over medium-high heat until hot, but not boiling, stirring to dissolve the sugar. Remove the pan from the heat and let the mixture cool slightly.

5. In a small bowl, whisk together the eggs and yolks until well blended. Slowly pour the eggs into the heated milk mixture, whisking constantly. Stir in the vanilla extract.

6. Place the ramekins in a baking pan and divide the milk mixture among the prepared ramekins. Add boiling water to the pan to come about 3/4 of the way up the sides of the ramekins. Bake the custards in the water bath for 35 to 45 minutes, or until they no longer tremble when moved.

7. Remove the ramekins from the pan, cool, and refrigerate, covered, for 3 to 4 hours.

8. To serve, unmold custards by running a knife around the edge of the ramekins and transfer onto dessert plates.

VARIATION: ESPRESSO FLAN

The flan recipe can easily be converted to a coffee-flavored version by adding 1 to 2 tablespoons powdered espresso, to taste, to the heated milk mixture and stirring until it is dissolved.

Fruit Liquados

Celebration **BEVERAGES**

Serving beverages at the Cooking School provides an opportunity to expose guests to the wine and beer being produced in New Mexico, which is the oldest wine-producing region in the United States. Wine production here dates back to the arrival of the Spanish in the 16th century, some eighty years prior to the arrival of the Pilgrims at Plymouth Rock. The original use of wine was for sacramental purposes, with the grapevine cuttings having been transported from Spain via Mexico up the El

Camino Real. Grapes were grown intermittently quite successfully throughout much of New Mexico's history. A series of natural influences, including drought and floods, weakened the wine industry, but the final demise of commercial wine activity was prohibition in 1920. Wine production reappeared in a minor way in the mid-'70s and has since grown into an industry with 18 licensed wineries producing well over a millions gallons per year. Many of the wines are nationally acclaimed.

The microbrewing industry has a much more recent history. The first commercial microbrewery started in 1988 with the Santa Fe Brewing Company, most noted for its Santa Fe Pale Ale. The state now has nine microbreweries.

At some of our special classes or events, we serve sangria and non-alcoholic beverages. Non-alcoholic beverages include fresh fruit drinks, or liquados, which can be seen throughout Mexico being sold from markets and street vendors. A multitude of fruit combinations and variations are possible, and these drinks make a delightfully refreshing beverage. The School's Breakfast class provides a good opportunity for serving Mexican Hot Chocolate. Also included is a "remedios" tea recipe from Sylvia Vergara, a northern New Mexican farmer and food processor.

THE JAKE WEST MELON

Many fresh fruit drinks involve melon, and the Santa Fe Farmer's Market offers a wide variety of melons from which to choose. One of the first stalls which you see as you enter the Farmer's Market is a flatbed trailer full of large, round, ripe melons of all varieties, including a Jake melon named after Jake West, a farmer from Ft. Sumner who makes a trip with his melons every Tuesday and Saturday. Ft. Sumner is approximately 150 miles southeast of Santa Fe and is at an elevation of 4,000 feet, roughly 3,000 feet lower than Santa Fe. Jake believes the climate and the soil, rich in potassium, magnesium, and calcium, are the key factors in producing what is locally considered the most flavorful melons.

Strawberry-Lime Liquados

MAKES 4 CUPS

2 pints ripe strawberries, hulled and halved

1/2 cup fresh lime juice

1 cup cold water

Sugar to taste

1. Place the strawberries, lime juice, and water in the blender. Blend and add sugar to taste. Serve chilled.

Watermelon Liquados

SERVES 4

3 cups ripe watermelon chunks, seeded

1 cup cold water

Sugar to taste

1. Place watermelon chunks in a blender with the cold water. Blend until smooth. Add sugar to taste. Blend again and serve chilled.

Cantaloupe Liquados

MAKES 4 CUPS

3 cups ripe cantaloupe chunks

1 cup cold water

Sugar to taste

Fresh lime juice (optional)

1. Place cantaloupe, water, and sugar in a blender and puree. Taste and adjust sweetness. Add lime juice if you prefer a tart-sweet cooler. Serve chilled.

SOUTH OF THE BORDER LIQUADOS

Liquados in Santa Fe are made with water. In Mexico, milk is often substituted for the water, which makes the beverage similar to what is called a fruit smoothy in the United States.

Jamaica Liquados

MAKES 2 QUARTS

2 cups dried Jamaica or hibiscus blossoms

2 1/2 quarts water

Sugar to taste

Fresh lime juice to taste

1. Place the dried blossoms in the water and bring to a boil. Reduce the heat to a simmer and cook for 12 minutes. Add sugar to taste and balance with fresh lime juice. Serve chilled.

JAMAICA

Incorrectly presumed to be Jamaica flowers or dried hibiscus flowers, these are not really "blossoms" at all, but the calyx of the flowers before they open. They give Red Zinger tea its slightly acidic, refreshing quality and deep crimson color. They can be found in health food stores or specialty stores as "jamaica" or "flores de jamaica." The "J" is pronounced as an "H."

Sangria

**YIELD:
10 TO 12 SERVINGS**

1 cup sugar

1 cup water

1 cup freshly squeezed
lime juice

1 1/2 cups freshly
squeezed orange juice

3 1/2 cups red or
white wine

1 cup sparking water

1 lime, thinly sliced
into rounds

1 lemon, thinly sliced
into rounds

1 orange, thinly sliced
into half rounds

Fresh mint sprigs
for garnish

Sangria is a refreshing drink typically made with Spanish red wine, citrus fruit, brandy, and club soda. This version eliminates the brandy, but you won't miss it.

1. Place the sugar and the water in a small saucepan and bring to a boil. Continue to boil until the sugar has dissolved and the syrup is clear, about 10 minutes.
2. In a large container, combine the fruit juices and sugar syrup, and mix well.
3. Add the wine, sparkling water, and sliced fruit and allow to sit for 10 minutes. Serve in wine glasses over ice garnished with some of the sliced fruit. Garnish with a sprig of fresh mint.

Te De Ajo (Garlic Tea)

3/4 cup water (preferably pure mountain spring water or a very high-quality bottled water)

2 tablespoons La Carreta garlic vinegar (See Note)

1 tablespoon honey (preferably a honey that is local to your area)

OPTIONAL:

1 small slice of fresh, organic lemon or lime.

1 sprig of fresh, organic mint (Sylvia uses a type of mint called Yerba Buena, which means the "good herb" and which grows wild in New Mexico.)

This is a remedios, or a remedy tea which Sylvia Vergara of La Carreta has made at the Cooking School Vendors' Day. Sylvia recommends this tea for calming down prior to retiring for the evening.

1. Boil the water in a tea kettle. Pour into your favorite cup.

2. Add the garlic vinegar and then add the honey. All the ingredients can be varied according to your taste. If you like strong tea, increase the amount of garlic vinegar. If you like your tea more delicate, decrease all the ingredients except the water.

NOTE:

La Carreta garlic vinegar is an authentic aged vinegar made from fresh-pressed, organic apple cider. It is sulfite free, contains no salts or sugars and is not diluted with water. You can make your own garlic vinegar by taking fresh, organic garlic and adding it to a high-quality apple cider vinegar and letting it sit in a closed jar for at least two weeks before using.

MAKING THE BEST PRESERVES (TIP FROM SYLVIA VERGARA)

When making preserves, always select fruits by tasting them first, and then by their appearance. A piece of fruit might look beautiful but have no flavor. For optimum flavor and color, carefully schedule your fruit delivery or purchase. Have your farmer pick the fruit the day you will make the preserves. Fruits that go directly from the tree into the jar make the best preserves.

VENDORS' DAY

At least once a year, we have a Vendors' Day at the Cooking School. I invite local food processors to give demonstrations on the use of their products in creating quick and easy tasty treats. These free demonstrations have been well received. Two of the largest food processors in the state are Santa Fe Seasons and Santa Fe Olé, who offer a large selection of products which can be used for shortcuts in the preparation of Southwestern food. The Vendors' Day at the Cooking School always includes these companies because they offer such extensive and high-quality products. Smaller companies are also invited to participate, and they play an important part at the Cooking School.

Spiced Coffee

YIELD: 6 CUPS

6 cups water

4 ounces piloncillo, or 1/2 cup dark brown sugar, packed

2 3-inch pieces canela

10 whole cloves

2 3-inch pieces orange peel, pith removed

3/4 cup coarsely ground dark-roasted coffee

Milk or cream (optional)

1. Combine the water, piloncillo, canela, cloves, and orange peel in a saucepan over medium-high heat and bring to a boil. Reduce heat to low, cover the pan, and steep for 5 minutes, stirring occasionally.
2. Remove the pan from the heat, add the coffee, and let it steep, covered, for 10 minutes. Strain the coffee through a sieve lined with a double layer of cheese-cloth into a warm coffee pot or pitcher. Serve immediately with milk or cream.

Mexican Hot Chocolate

SERVES 2

1 1/2 ounces Mexican chocolate, such as Ibarra (See Mexican Chocolate)

1 1/4 cups milk

1/4 cup heavy cream

Whipped cream (optional)

Canela sticks (Mexican cinnamon) for garnish

If you have never tasted hot chocolate made with Mexican chocolate such as Ibarra, you are in for a treat. Mexican chocolate is also used extensively in Santa Fe-style cooking. It is available in Hispanic markets, or through mail order.

1. Chop the chocolate and place it in a blender.
2. In a small, heavy pot, bring the milk and heavy cream just to a boil. Immediately pour the hot milk into the blender and blend until the chocolate is thoroughly blended and the mixture is frothy.
3. Pour the liquid into cups, top with whipped cream, if desired, and garnish with canela sticks.

VARIATION:

If you cannot locate Mexican chocolate, substitute a similar quantity of semi-sweet chocolate along with a pinch of canela or cinnamon.

MEXICAN CHOCOLATE

The Aztecs so revered chocolate that it was reserved for kings and priests, who used it in a potent ceremonial drink. Chicahuatl, a special beverage that was made by combining chiles and chocolate, might have been the Aztecs' contribution to Mexican chocolate which is spiced with cinnamon, vanilla, and crushed almonds. Ibarra Mexican chocolate is the brand most commonly found in the United States. Real Mexican hot chocolate enthusiasts use a molinillo, a decoratively notched stick that is vigorously rubbed between the hands, for frothing up the chocolate mixture while it is heating.

Farmers market in Santa Fe

WHERE TO FIND IT: *Sources for*

Southwestern Ingredients

SANTA FE SCHOOL OF COOKING MARKET

116 W. San Francisco St.

Santa Fe, NM 87501

(505) 983-4511

Large variety of dried chiles, fresh New Mexican green chiles shipped in season (July, August, and September), chile seeds, full range of New Mexican and Southwestern ingredients and seasonings, Southwestern cooking equipment. Catalog available.

PASTORES LAMB

P.O. Box 118

Los Ojos, NM 87551

1-800-321-5262

Churro, Karakul, and Poquitero Lamb by the half or whole. Available from September through December. Shipped UPS.

LEONA'S DE CHIMAYO

P.O. Box 579

Chimayo, NM 87522

(800)-4LEONAS

Tortillas. Traditional flour, whole wheat and flavored. Tamales.

SWEETWOODS DAIRY

P.O. Box 1238 Peña Blance, NM 87041

505-465-2608

Goat cheese made fresh daily. Plain and herb flavored.

NATIVE SEEDS/SEARCH

2509 N. Campbell Ave. #325

Tucson, AZ 85719

Variety of seeds of the Southwestern Native American crops.

EMBUDO SMOKEHOUSE

P.O. Box 154

Embudo, NM 87531

1-800-852-4707

Smoked turkeys, hams, trout, bacon, and ribs.

LA CARRETA

Box 70

Dixon, NM 87527

(505) 579-4358

Preserves, sauces, syrups, and vinegars.

RANCHO CASADOS

P.O. Box 1149

San Juan Pueblo, NM 87566

(505) 852-4482

Fresh and processed regional foods.

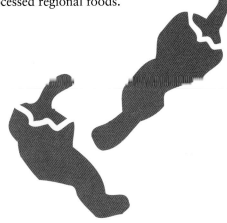

INDEX

If you would like to receive information about the Santa Fe School of Cooking and Market, please copy and fill out this form and mail it to:

THE SANTA FE SCHOOL OF COOKING

116 WEST SAN FRANCISCO STREET

SANTA FE, NEW MEXICO 87501

Please check the type of mailing you would like to receive.

☐   **PRODUCT CATALOG**

☐   **CLASS SCHEDULE**

☐   **EXTENDED PROGRAM OR CULINARY TOUR**

☐   **FRESH GREEN CHILE ORDER FORMS**
     (Available August and September)

☐   **ALL MAILINGS FROM THE SANTA FE SCHOOL
     OF COOKING**

NAME _____

ADDRESS _____

CITY _____**STATE** _____

PHONE _____